Collected Works

Wealthy Odessa (Rainwater) Calvert

Biography

Wealthy Odessa (Rainwater) Calvert known as Aunt Wealthy was born June 30, 1908 in Montreal, Missouri to Everette and Betty (Head) Rainwater. She married Thomas Egbert Calvert on March 18, 1937.

Wealthy was a poet at heart and passed along volumes of poems and songs to her loved ones and church family. She was a correspondent for the local newspapers and had many poems published in the Reveille and Miller County Autogram.

She could play any musical instrument she picked up and those who knew her knew she always had her "harp" (harmonica) with her and a song in her heart.

Additionally, she loved the outdoors, especially working in her beautiful flowers and vegetable garden. She was a caring neighbor and friend and always wanted to share the bounty of her hands

Wealthy passed away at the age of 100 on Sunday, April 26, 2009 at the Windsor Estates Nursing Home in Camdenton, Missouri.

Contents

Birthdays...151

Family and Friends 163

Nature

My Ozark Valley Home

There's a little green valley that I love,
Away down in the hills.
Where flowers bloom with sweet perfume
And little birds sing and build

Where whippoorwills call at even tide,
And wake in the morn.
It's a place that is home sweet home to me
The place where I was born

A place where nature opens her doors
And throws away the key,
And lets a child of hers come in,
To wonder and be free.

It's spring time again in the valley,
In every bud and flower
In every breeze that's blowing,
In every little shower.

I love to peep in dew kissed buds
Unfolding in the sun.
Breathe pure fragrant zephyrs
When day has just begun.

Where all of nature in her newness
Where God is such a friend,
Where inspiration incarnated
In my soul with beauty blends.

In shady nooks where it's cool and quiet
And heaven's not far above,
Just listening in to nature's program,
All in harmony and love.

Oh, I love to be in the spring time
Away down in the hills
In my little green Ozark valley
With the birds and flowers and whippoorwills.

Wealthy's Ozark Valley Home with her mother on the porch

Untitled Work, April 1, 1999

The pretty roses that are blooming,
With all their colors bright and fair
It could not unfold such beauty,
Without its sweet fragrance to share.

Our lives are made a little richer
By the deeds that we do.
Tho' they may be small and unnoticed
Often unseen by so few,

Yet that love that we planted
Like the fragrance in the rose
Our kindness will be remembered
Perhaps by some one that we know

Untitled Work, October 31, 1998

How sweet is the quietness
After a storm has passed by
When the clouds have all departed
And again we see the beauty in the sky

When nature returns to quietness
Its then our hearts are made glad
In the protection to us God has given
In his love for us he has had

My life's memories will be like bridges
That others will often cross
May the examples that I practiced
Be safe steps for others to cross

The Sunset

In all the ugliness we have seen
In our winter close of days
But oh this evening there was such a beauty
In the sunset so far away

After all the cold and wintery ugliness
That we have had to fight
But oh this evening I saw such a beauty
In the sunset far away in my sight

I felt the presence and touch of God
In his great love, beauty, and concern
To share with a world that's in sin and hatred
If only the people to him would turn

Then I thought of all God's blessings
He longs to share with the human race
If they would only turn from sin and Satan
And let God's love and honor be replaced

February 13, 1996

April Nights

Down the valley I hear the whip-poor-will's plaintiff cry
When the evening sun is low
In patches of darkness there flickers a light
From the fireflies dynamo
The twinkling stars peep down and glitter
They seem to smile and say
"Oh, you little vales and hills How quiet at the close of day"
A dew from heights, unfathomed, untouched
Nestles down in new born buds
A responsive nature takes her gentle walk

When there's nothing to disturb
The moon climbs high to her place in the heavens
And unfolds her mellow light
An x-ray of nature we then behold
In a silent springtime night
Oh, you little green valleys and Ozark hills
With your air so pure and free
With nights that are quiet where nature sojourns
In the place that's home to me

The Voice of a Little Dove

The other day somewhere I heard
The soft cooing of a little dove
Then in my heart came a message
That spoke to me in the sweetest love

So many times in God's Bible
This little bird has its name
And each time its been mentioned
There's been an honor to be proclaimed

Wealthy at her home near Montreal, Missouri

Index to Spring

A – is for air with odors of Spring, fresh plowed fields, grasses, and rain

B – is for the birds with sweet songs, building their nests all day long

C – is for crocuses awakening from sleep, when a warm shower tickles at their sleep

D – is for daffodils, like nuggets of gold, hid among grasses so yellow and bold

E – is for Easter that we all know, because it was the day our Lord arose

F – is for the frost that sometimes comes, and kills the berries, peaches and plums

G – is for the grasses, earth's carpet of green, on hills in valleys everywhere to be seen

H – is for the hawthorn clustered with blooms, white and delicate as a bride in June

I – is for the iris, we all admire, in everybody's yard nearly everywhere

J – is for the jonquil, a sunny little bloom, that makes us forget the winter's gloom

K – is for the kiss of warm rains, that restores the earth to beauty again

L – is for the lizards too lazy to run, after taking a bath in the first warm sun

M – is for the mushrooms, pushing out of the ground, so good to eat when fried nice and brown

N – is for the nights with a big bright moon, shining to set all nature in tune

O – is for the orchards, all fragrant and pink, with bees sipping nectar as quick as a wink

P – is for potatoes, and as we all know, often get nipped by a frost or snow

Q – is for the quail, our bobwhite friend, that lets us know when spring begins

R – is for the roses, just beginning to peep, from green little buds so waxy and sweet

S – is for the sun, climbing over the hill, warming the earth from dews and chill

T – is for the trees swaying in the wind, with leafy boughs for birds to nest in

U – is for the utterance of nature to man, in seasons language, that we all understand

V – is for vegetables, lettuce, carrots, and beans, and all the other good things growing between

W – is for the wind, mother nature's broom, to sweep off leaves for little early blooms

X – is for the x-ray on a moon light night, over the beautiful old earth so perfect and quiet

Y – is for the yawn at break of day, when songbirds awake us singing so gay

Z – is for the zephyrs bringing sweet refrains, to let us know its spring time again

March 1980

Alone with Nature

I strolled along one evening
Down a path with Ozark hills,
'Midst the loveliness of the springtime,
My heart with happiness filled.

Alone with nature and with God,
Down isles of sweetest peace,
I paused and mused and listened
To the language in release.

I breathed the purest sweetest breezes,
Laden with rich perfume,
Gathered from nature's vials
From the flowers that were in bloom.

White ones, red ones, yellow, pink, and blue,
All perfect in design;
A touching of Nature's fingerprints
On everyone I'd find.

Birds would fly 'mong tall tree branches,
Chirp and sing their songs;

Cool, clear brooks 'long side of the hill,
Babbled and ran on.

Nature's doors seemed to stand ajar,
There were no locks and keys;
All was peace, a bit of perfection,
All in love with harmony.

Sunbeams played through leaves and branches.
All nature was at home;
And I, as her guest,
Just happily strolled along.

Away from cares that weigh the soul,
And mar God's natural laws,
In a realm of life in Nature's bliss,
I sang and strolled and paused.

Assured that life can be sweetened
And while here this soul of mine
Can foretaste of that perfection
Of a life that'll be divine

My Feathered Friends

I've been watching out my window,
For my little feathered friends.
That come when spring flowers were blooming,
And staying till summer ends.

I haven't seen them for several days,
But yet, I look to see.
For I loved my little feathered friends,
That seemed so happy and free.

But I guess Mother Nature,
Whispered in each tiny ear.
Told them was time to Southward,
For winter would soon be here.

I never heard them singing,
Like most the birds I knew.
But I loved that humming in their wings,
As only humming birds can do.

I loved to watch their playful antics,
As they flitted all around.
And sipped in my feeders,
That they so easily found.

Hanging on my porch their sweetness.
That I placed there each day.
They were there in early morning,
And till dark they would stay.

But Mother Nature has her way,
To tell them when to go.
Where there is a warmer place,
Our Ozark winter is just too cold.

So I'll put away their feeders,
May even shed a tear.
For I loved the little hummers,
And miss them when not here.

My Little Green Valley

There's a little green valley that I love
Away down in the hills,
Where flowers bloom in sweet perfume
And little birds sing and build.

A valley that cradled all my dreams
From childhood thru the years,
And kept each memory that I cherished
And helped me hide my tears.

A valley where Mother was at home
Till God called her one day,
And now it holds all the memories
Of things she'd do and say.

There's an old green cedar on the hill
That's braved many a storm,
Thru all the ice and wind and rain
Never a branch was torn.

There's the spring of water, clear and cold
Flowing lazily along its way,
Where many times has quenched my thirst
In the heat of summer days.

The old grapevine that never failed
That grew on the side of the hill,
The little wren that always came
On the porch her nest to build.

The yard was full of pretty flowers
That bloomed the year around,
And just about every kind
Was there to be found.

There's the places where I prayed
And places where I cried,
But thru all my joys and sorrows
The Lord was by my side.

But time did come when I had to go
And fairer skies to find,
Build and dream at other scenes
And leave the valley behind.

Maybe when the earth is all made new
With no sin, or parting, or pain,
God will have me a little mansion
And give me back my valley again.

By Wealth (Rainwater) Calvert, Richland, MO

Little Birds

Today I stood looking out my window
Some little birds were hopping 'round
I just watched them in their care free way
As they skipped across the ground.

Now and then they seemed to gather
A tiny seed or a little bite to eat
Just what it was I could not see
But to them, it seemed to be a treat

But as I watched them I remembered
What the Bible has to say
how God feeds the little birds
Is mindful of them every day

I thot how he placed the little seeds
And in winters dry and withered grass
He knew where there'd be a hungry bird
That would soon or later pass

They do not ask for granaries full
Or large storage bins

But just a seed or crumb each day
Makes a hearty meal for them

So let's not forget our feathered friends
When the snow and cold must come
God may ask you and I to provide
For them a little seed or crumb

Beauty in the Storm (of November 20, 1988) _"Beauty in the Storm". I got these words that came to me, after I saw the beautiful snow scene last Sunday morning._

That beautiful snow Sunday morning
Was a picture to behold
Only nature could place those snowflakes
In such beauty to unfold.

Made me think of God's salvation
When he made my soul white as snow
Thru the shed blood of his dear son
On Calvary's cross, so long ago.

Brought to my mind new inspirations
To my eyes more beauty see
To my heart a new rejoicing
A deeper faith in him, received.

As I stood looking from my window
Like tiny bubbles, I could see
Their many bright colors flashing
Among the snowflakes in the trees.

From this snow covered scene I visioned
The complete salvation plan
How the cleansing blood of God's own son
Makes white the soul from every man.

As I walked away from my window
In my soul there was a voice
I had seen the master's touch again
And my heart was made to rejoice

Hodgepodge

Greetings

So many times when folks are sick
I'm without a card with a get well wish
But that does not mean that's the end
For me to remember my shut in friends

God has given me a great big heart
And filled it with love for me to impart
And in the depths of this love so rich and fine
I can always find wishes for friends of mine

Wishes that are tender
And warm and true
Just the kind that's needed
By folks like you

So I searched my heart
In tenderest care
And my soul was humbled
In sincere prayer

That the wish that was chosen
Would not be mine
But the one God has for you
For this particular time

One I can pass on
Fragrant with his love
Enveloped in beauty
From Heaven above

One that will hover
O're you like wings
And great power of healing
To you bring

Our Riches

So often the days on life's journey,
The clouds over spread the sky,
And the way seems long and dreary,
Long anxious hours pass us by.

Like flowers that lose their fragrance,
And song birds that cease to sing,
Life too will seemingly lose its beauty,
With shattered hopes and broken dreams.

Sometimes a smile will move the cloud,
That hangs so heavy and dark,
Changing the drab threads I life's loom,
To beautiful shining spots.

Perhaps a word of kindness spoken
Will fall life fluffy down
Upon a broken bleeding heart
And sooth the aching pounds.

A little encouragement from someone,
Who has seen our darkening cloud,
Will sometime change a whole day thru,
And lift the black like shroud.

We don't always know the worth of smiles,
We give to others every day,
Or what a happy greeting means
That we send along the way.

Simple bouquets we sometimes give,
Of some half scented flowers
We never know how bright they bloom,
In someone's lonely hours.

So as we go along life's way,
Meeting each day's new scene
Remember, it's one of our duties,
To scatter some sunshine between.

To scatter bouquets for happiness,
Give riches, not of silver and gold,
By little deed that are priceless,
To heal the hurts some hearts hold.

The Price of a "Thank You"

Just a thank you don't always pay
For a job that is well done
There's always an expense involved
On behalf of some thoughtful one

It's nice to have a helping hand
From someone so good and kind
But some time just a thank you
Don't repay for their cost and time

Yes, how precious are the ones
That are so thoughtful of me
In my reclining years with age
With many needs whatever they be

So many times I fail to count
The cost that is involved
In the kindly things that are done
To help in problems I can't solve

Whatever in life my needs may be
One thing I can share
Is a love I have for those
Who stand by me and care

May I too be a blessing
And find someone along my way
That I can help lift their burden
Because of help you gave me one day

A Memorial to 1993 Apples

To be sure this is the last one
Of the big good apples on the tree
Mother Nature has been so good and kind
To share her best with you and me

So what ever the seasons may now bring
In the years that lie ahead
May we always have its apples
Till the tree, or you and I are dead

October 27, 1993

1994

The pace of time with all its advancements
Are becoming far beyond our limitations
The true values for the coming century
Will be absorbed by mans technology and intervention

The bounds of human experimentation
Will seem to have no end
With its sale price for promotion
For future power, for greed and gain

Human minds will be absorbed
With a wisdom that was never known
The laws of God will be abused
Many perhaps will become unknown

The lusts of sins will have new meaning
And become a way of life
Guilt will be erased by lust and fashion
Conscience free, become the price

Scientific technology invades our generation
With its limit to deceive
Satan again will try to restore his promises
That first were made in Eden's garden to Eve

However all these hastened changes
Are being fulfilled in technology's mind
But God's warnings have been made known
In the very days of our time

Satan again has took advantage
With his wisdom and his pride
For greed and gain and lust and power
God's laws are being shoved aside

The mind of men has become absorbed
For a knowledge beyond his power
And Satan has again took advantage
And wickedness is the reward for this hour

But the people who are called by God's name
And are inspired by his love
And have received his gift of salvation
Have been redeemed by Christ's shed blood

The Ozarks of Missouri

There was a time when old Missouri
Scarcely thought she was a state,
Dreaming only of hill-billies,
As her long and future fate.

Thinking that her hills and valleys
Were a blemish on her name,
Never dreaming that some day
They would bring her wealth and fame.

She didn't know she would be honored
By a dam across her streams
To cradle in her arms the Ozark lake,
A wonder beauty, woven dream.

She didn't know she was possessed
With a land of a million smiles,
Smiles that grew so broad
They'd reach for thousands of miles.

And bring her daily visitors,
Who would gaze in admiration
Upon her hills, flowers and streams
And her handiwork of nature.

But now it's become a slogan
To "See Missouri First,"
And if you'll watch the traffic,
You'll believe is sure enough.

Almost like a daily picnic
Everyday around her lake,
Fishing, swimming and boat riding,
She holds the world at stake.

She has her roads, schools and churches,
She's decked with berries and good fruit,
Jersey cows to make the cream,
Pork and beans and eggs to boot.

She's just nature's freakish garden
Of the Master's own design,
Another emblem of the union
That the people are just now finding.

So pack up your troubles for an airing
And come to the Ozark land.
Enjoy your summer's vacation
With the rest of the touring band.

Bring your fishing poles along,
Fish right in the lake,
Rent you a cabin or camp for a week
And a real vacation take
In the Ozarks of Missouri.

When the Huntin' Season is Over

Bunny rabbit was hopping along one day,
When he met with an old friend,
Mr. 'Possum with his friendly words,
And his usual happy grin.

I'm very happy today, he said
I'm sure that you are too.
Folks will quit huntin' for us
The huntin' seasons through.

Oh yes, shouted the little bunny,
You bet I'm happy indeed,
I've had to stay out of my den
Till I'd nearly freeze.

A little ol' boy with squinty eyes,
Came to my den one day,

And set some old rusty traps,
When I was gone away.

It was dark when I came back,
I did not look around
And into my den I went,
When I heard an awful sound.

I just barely tripped his trap,
Oh, I heard it ring,
How near I set my feet,
On that old rusty spring.

Oh, yeah my little friend,
The 'Possum said very quiet,
They took my den with all the others,
And hunted for me at night.

An ol' hound caught me once,
But I finally got away,
And ran into a cave near by,
And I heard the hunters say,

We'll come tomorrow and set a trap
And then when he comes out,
We'll play a trick on that lad,
We'll get the little scout.

But I did not stay till morning,
I left some time that night,
And I am very thankful now,
That I got by alright.

We poor dumb animals have a time,
The 'Possum said and sighed,

They treat us, oh so cruel,
Just to get our hides.

Then the ladies act so proud,
Pimped up in our pelts,
They never care how we suffer,
They never know that pains we felt.

But tonight, said the bunny,
We can shelter where we please.
Aren't you glad that there's an end,
To this awful huntin' lease?

Air Pollution (Number One)

I hear so much about air pollution
Till it nearly makes me sick
But you never hear a word about in the homes
Where cigarette smoke gets so thick

Take about any kind of gathering
When people gather up around
And they all get lit up good
With all their different smoking brands

Talk about a halo 'round your head
Circling to the ceiling
With a film that plasters all your senses
And your lungs get a plugged up feeling

The odor that penetrates our clothing
And lingers in our hair
It just over comes all the freshness
That God put in his clean, fresh air.

(P.S.) Maybe I am just to old fashion
Oh, no I am not an old crank
I just can't take cigarette smoke
I just want pure air and give God the thanks.

January 1993

A Criminal's Love Letter

I was walking one day
Down the highway alone
Caring for nobody
The law, friends or home.

I was running away
From crimes I had done
Dodging the sheriff
Disgracing loved ones.

My heart was as black
As an evening shade
And hard and cold
As they ever made.

I walked thru the tears,
My mother had shed,
And trampled the prayers
For me she had said.

The Bible she placed
In my pocket one day,
I tore it in pieces
And threw it away.

I thought it was smart
To be in some crime,

Dodging the sheriff,
Or pay out a fine.

But as I was sneaking along
One particular day,
I found a package,
Lying beside my way.

It was wrapped up so pretty,
Tied so neat and nice,
I thought it must be something
Worth a good price.

I snatched it quickly
I darted for the brush,
I walked quite a distance,
From sight, noise and dust.

I hid behind a big oak tree,
I sat down on the ground,
Very quietly I unwrapped it,
To see what I had found.

A silence came about me,
All creation seemed to hush,
A presence seemed to touch me,
As I sat there in the brush.

There in letters that seemed to sparkle,
Flared right up in my eyes,
It was a Holy Bible,
The book I had despised.

It seemed to cling to my hands,
It was so white and new,

And a note inside the cover,
Said, "Please read me thru."

I knew this note had not been written
Just for me to read,
But somehow as I read it,
I wanted to take heed.

I started turning thru its pages,
Just to pass the time away,
Here and there I'd read a verse,
Just to see what they did say.

Then a breeze blew the pages,
To the 3rd Chapter of John,
And the 16th verse stood out clear,
Where my eyes fasted on.

I read it through a dozen times,
Each time I seemed to see,
The Son of God nailed to the cross
And looking down at me.

I fell down upon my face,
I cried, "Oh, Lord Devine".
Is it for me you're dying there
For a criminal soul like mine?

Then other verses that I'd read,
Each one I seemed to see,
Each one spoke of love,
That God had for me.

I felt a great sharp conviction,
Deep in my stony heart,

I felt a great guilt and shame,
That tore me all apart.

I could see myself a criminal,
From the laws I had to dodge,
I could see myself a sinner,
And far away from God.

I began to cry, and oh, how bitter
Were the tears that I shed,
I knew the Lord had spoke to me,
From his word that I read.

I clasped the Bible to my breast,
That was so white and new,
I cried, "Lord make me as clean,
By thy blood, thru and thru."

In my heart there came a peace,
I knew I was born again,
I felt his tough in cleansing power,
A criminal saved from sin.

Then I started home to my mother,
I was a different son,
All her prayers I'd trampled down,
God had heard every one.

And when I reached,
My dear old home,
My mother was standing,
In the door alone.

"Oh, Mother, I've come,
These words to say,

I got a love letter,
From Heaven today."

It was God's holy word,
So sweet and divine,
It made me to see,
That guilt of mine.

Now I'm on my way,
My Savior to see,
Who died on the cross,
For a sinner like me.

September 1955

Precious Things

The smile of innocent children
As they look into my face
I see some thing that God has given
His love and infinite grace

Beautiful sunsets at close of day
That I so often see
Reminds me of a fairer land
It's loveliness for all eternity

On and on I could never number
All of life's lovely things
That God has placed along my pathway
To erase the ugliness, trials often bring

Mother's Blue Star

The little blue star in my window
Has been changed to silver bright

God has hung it up in Heaven
And I see in there tonight

Neath a blue sky it is shining
As I gaze at it so bright
Like the bright stars in old glory
Sends a beacon thru the night

Tho' my darling now lies buried
In a land so far away
With a cross that marks this clay mound
Yet I seem to hear him say

"Mother's blue star has turned to silver
God has hung it up in the sky
Just an emblem of your soldier
Please dear mother, don't you cry"

Aunt Molly

A dear little lady, crippled and old
Aunt Molly, as she was known
Lived by her self, at the side of the road
In her own little humble home

Birds always sang around her lawn
And built among the trees
Flowers bloomed around her door
Where every one could see

Her days were started with a prayer
And always full of song
She took her Bible from its shelf
And read when the day was gone

She was known by all far and near
For her sweet and sunny life
For the kind of mother she had been
A true and saintly wife

Now her family all was gone
She had carried a heavy load
But she gave the best she had left
As she loved alone by the side of the road

She would always have an answer
And it seemed to be just right
She knew what to say to those in trouble
How to part their darkest night

Children passing by her door
Loved Aunt Molly's smile
Listened to hear her say "Come in"
And talk to me awhile

Her cookie jar was never empty
Cookies with colors and designs
The children just delighted
In looking for their kinds

Her friends always remembered
As they were passing by
To stop, if just for a minute
And just say hello or good bye

Usually they'd bring a little gift
All prettied up and neat
Or a dish of food or fruit
Something they knew she could eat

At Christmas time her crippled hands
Never found an idle minute
For every one she'd write a greeting
From Aunt Mol, she would sign it

She'd place them in a little basket
That she had trimmed so bright
And every one knew they had a greeting
In Aunt Molly's own hand write

But one morning there was a quietness
At the house beside the road
Neighbors heard no one singing
Some thing wrong they surely knowed

When they enter in her door way
There they saw her on her bed
With her Bible by her side
Dear Aunt Molly, was lying dead

Her crippled hands had left a note
And this is what it said
"Good bye, I love you all
I now must go to bed"

"I am going home tonight dear friends
My work on earth now is o'er
I am going now to join my family
On that bright and happy shore"

"You all have made my life so sweet
I thank you, every one
I'll be looking for your coming
Just like I always have done"

"Children, the cookie jar is full
Of goodies I left for you
Come on in and find your kinds
Just like you always do"

"May God bless your little hands
That reached into my cookie jar
We'll meet again some day in Heaven
And I'll yet remember who you are"

A Tribute

Today, we are gathered together, the off spring of a generation, another century of time.

We look back thru the long years to the time when Buffalo's roamed across the fields and hills, which rightfully gave this community the name of Buffalo Prairie.

We see that first faithful little group of men and women who loved God, and had that earnest desire to worship Him. We see them as they sacrificed and worked together to build that first little log house, where they could meet and fellowship together. Here we see the first footprints that began the history of the Buffalo Prairie Baptist Church.

We see the faith where on this first place of worship was built. It's foundation embedded in love and anchored on the solid Rock Jesus Christ, himself.

Yes, we see the footprints of many struggles, many failures, but that faith of a few consecrated men and women who stood true and stalwart in every battle and saw the victory gained for the Lord and his church.

Across our country many monuments mark the grave of dear saints who are pillars in the history of the Buffalo Prairie Baptist Church, as it stands today.

We have seen the progress of time and God's blessings upon it. Thru a century of years, it has stood as a light house to guide and lead lost and wayward souls, to find Jesus Christ, as their personal Savior.

Today, as we see our church building with all its beauty and modern conveniences, we yet see the sacrifices and labor, of faithful men and women who love God, and have that earnest desire to keep it a place of worship. A place, where the Holy Bible can be proclaimed in all its truth and purity and lost souls be won for Christ. A place of Fellowship, to help bear one another's burdens.

So today, let us rededicate our lives and continue to build on that faith that laid the foundation for that first little humble log church house, that was built on Buffalo Prairie a century ago.

May our prayer always be that this faith and spirit of love continue to prosper and nourish the Buffalo Prairie Baptist Church and preserve it, for the generations yet to come, or until the Lord returns for His own.

By Wealthy Calvert, Montreal, Mo.

A True Story

I believe I have a prize winning story, or at least it's one I can pass on. Friday evening must been round 2 o'clock I went out to open the door to my well house, as the temperature was so hot inside. I had a big piece of thick board that I leaned against the door. I usually push this board to the ground when I go inside the well house, but this evening, I just opened the door back, stepped inside, and as I did, the thick board stayed against the door, and closed it. Of course the more I pushed against the door the tighter it closed the door. I tried to break the door and no way could I get the door to give an inch. I did manage to have a short piece of a 2x4 there in the well house that I forced between the top of the door and the wall, which gave me a little place for more air. I tried to pry the door up from the bottom with a shovel that was in the well house, but everything seemed to just tighten the door. I started yelling for help out the space the piece of 2x4 made. Every time I heard a car coming on the highway, below my house, I began yelling, "Help, help, some body help me." I didn't know if any one could hear me from the distance I was from the road and being inside a closed building . But after about 3 hours, God heard my prayer and prepared some one to hear me. I started hearing a motor running down on the road and I kept yelling help and pretty soon, I heard some one and I felt God was sending one to rescue me, and what a relief when some one opened the well house door. I was very exhausted, practically wet with sweat and nearly over come with heat. Who ever this fine gentleman was, he helped me to my house, offered any assistance he thot I might need, and my sincere thanks to him was "I thank the dear Lord for you." I know it had to be an answer to my faith in prayer that he was permitted to hear my call for help.

May this precious man, who ever he was, or where ever he is, be blessed richly for being used to save my life.

A true story by Wealth Calvert, Montreal Mo, R 1 Box 28, 65591 at the E and A junction, near Montreal, Mo. I will be 80 years old June 30. This happened 1988.

Untitled Work, No Date (1)

About twelve years ago, I had a mother hen to hatch a bunch of little chickens. One of these was a little white chickens and was different form all the rest. It was never anything but a little pet, and its unusual peculiarities soon won its place in my heart. And this naturally caused me to give her a lot my attention.

While very small, she liked to sit on my lap and be petted. She would sit and sleep, and stay as long as I cared to hold her, The older she grew the more intelligent she became.

When she wanted something to eat, or be petted, she'd fly over the yard gate and come to the porch and sing until she drew my attention. If I was sitting on the porch, she'd fly up on my lap and sing, or do her best to talk to me. I learned her to let me clean off her beak after she'd eat, and like a child, she responded to this attention. I'd often take her out around the place, and turn up rocks for her to find bugs and worms and she'd stay with me, very busy watching under everything I'd turn over.

When she was about five years old, we moved, and at that time there was no place for chickens at our new location, So I could not take her, which broke my heart. I left her with my sister - in-law, an she had a good home.

Every time I'd visit there, I'd go out and catch her, pet and feed her.

After a few months I got home sick for my little pet hen, and I fixed me a big chicken yard at the back of my house.

I bought six other hens, and went and got my little pet hen. She hadn't forgot me, and was soon adjusted and happy, with me again. In a short time she was coming to the yard gate and singing for me, when she wanted attention. She was also choicy about her eating, and among the things she liked best were milk, bread with sorghum mixed in, sauer kraut, lettuce and cooked beans. One day something got wrong with one of her eyes, and I thought it was going to kill her. She responded like a child to all the care and love I gave her, and never failed to always try to talk to me. However, her eye got well, but vision was impaired in it, but she continued healthy and happy.

About the first of January she became sick, and there seemed to be nothing I could do for her. I'd bring her in the house, and gave her the best care. Lettuce was about all she would eat. I'd pet her and talk to her and she'd lift her little pale head, look into my face and do her best to talk back to me. Often I'd be crying and she seemed to notice that something was wrong, as she'd look up at me.

As I stood be her crying, I had faith in God to believe he cared for a little hen, as much as any other part of his creation, and O humbly prayed, saying, "Lord shes just a little hen and always been good, and different, please, don't let her suffer." About five minutes passed and she quietly raised to her feet, moved her head, opened her eyes, and just eased back down in her sitting position, and died without a struggle. Later in the day, I placed her a little box and buried her, with tears falling upon her little grave.

I'm sure that God who understands all things, had a reason in the life of this little hen, that he gave me to love and care for, all these twelve years.

A true story by -
Mrs. Egbert Calvert
Montreal, Missouri

The Reporter's History's Corner

By Merle Cross

Chicken yard with no regulations

The late Aunt Wealthy (Rainwater) Calvert can be be seen feeding her chickens in 1947. This Rainwater homestead was located east of Montreal, Missouri. Aunt Wealthy said the old rooster usually crowed around 5 a.m. every morning. There were also two geese that ran with the chickens and a gander that would bite you on your leg if you turned your back. Many of us can reminisce of the days when receiving baby chicks by mail was common practice. What fun times! There were several brands of chickens such as Leghorns, Plymouth Rocks, New Hampshires and Rhode Island Reds just to name a few. (Photo courtesy of Merle Cross)

My Life's Play Pen

Words have always been my playthings
In the play pen of my life
And when I put them together rightly
They then gave me thoughts to write

I begin to call them inspirations
With a meaning in a rhyme
But I had to choose them wisely
To get a picture in my mind

Then I'd gather my thoughts together
Jot down a line or two
Repeat them over a few times then
To see what they would do

If I then could get a picture
That'd come to my mind
I'd call that an inspiration
For the right words to find

Many times I'd just sat thinking
In the play pen of my life
And I'd just look out my window
As I searched for a word to write

Life's play pen now is growing old
The words are faded and torn
Thru many years they've been such a pleasure
As I put many together in my poems

But some day when life's play pen is folded
And no more words I can find

But somewhere in some ones scrap book
There will yet be words that once were mine

In my new life I will understand
The meaning of my play pen words
Each inspiration will become a reality
With precious meaning I'd never heard

Some day the Lord will let me know
In that new life so pure and bright
I'll know why he chose my play pen words
With inspirations for things to write

Someday I will understand
When God's wisdom he will release
As I walk close to my Savior's side
And he talks to me on Heaven's golden streets

1992

Song Poems

When I Don't Understand

They're many things here in this life
That I don't understand
But it's not for me to question
God holds them in his hand

But when I walk some brighter morn
And on some fairer shore
With Jesus by my side I'll learn
The things that I don't know

When the storms are ranging wild
With high and boisterous tide
And when my strength is nearly gone
And my heart is broke inside

Just let me have the faith it takes
To meet each trying test
Just let me say "thy will be done"
My savior he knows best

I hear the words my master said
When the storm was on the sea
And the people how they cried to him
"Lord carest thou for me"

So let me hear that still small voice
When I don't understand
And lift my helpless self to him
And take him by the hand

"Peace be still "I hear him say
"My child I care for you
Just keep you r eyes upon the cross
And I will take you thru"

So as I meet the things of life
That I don't understand
It's not for me to question
God holds them in his hand

*I sang this with a tune that was given me and played my harmonica
as a special at church October 19, 1986. The Lord used it as a special
blessing in the service (I say, "Praise the Lord").*

Cold Love (A Song Poem)

I can't love you, tho' I call you darling
I'm just playing with your heart, teasing you
I don't want to make you promise
My heart won't let me love and be a friend that's true.

Your kisses are cold and has no meaning
When you hold me tightly in your embrace
I just resist your tender loving
Can't you see the blush on my face.

Can't you see with out me have to tell you
Your love is cold and chilling as a wind
How many times will I have to tell you
I'll be nobody's sweet heart again.

Your words of love are only wasted
That you whisper in my ear
For they are just like ice drops falling
Always melted before my heart can hear.

Yes, darling I know you love me
With a love that is true
But I can't give you your kind of loving
And do what you want me to do.

I have a sweet heart some where in Heaven
He's waiting and watching for me
Some day the pearly gates will swing open
And then his smiling face I'll see.

He will take me in his arms again
And kiss my tears away
Side by side, we'll walk together
Thru out Heaven's eternal day

Wasted Love - A Song Poem

1. Oh, the days are so lonely my darling
For its now that I know what you meant
And its now that you've broken my heart love
Left me thinking of days that we spent

Oft at night, as I sit by my window
With the mellow moonlight in my face
Gazing there thru my tears at your picture
For its all I have left in your place

2. Oh, I often do wonder my darling
Why it was that you came in my life
Like the dew on the roses at sunrise
You just vanished away from my sight

 All the things we had planned for our future
Now are crumpled and crushed in my heart
All my love that was true now is wasted
All my hopes and plans now must depart

3. But some say when your wanderings are over
And the silver has come in your hair
When the sunset of life overtakes you
Will you have some one then who will care

Little Moses

A Song in the Key of G#

Down by the water so clear
The maidens were winding their way
The fairest little daughter stepped down in
The water, to bathe in cool of the day
Before it was dark she opened the ark
And found a sweet infant were there

Away by the water so blue, the infant
Looks lonely and sad.
She took him in pity and that him pretty
It made little Moses so glad
She called him her own, her beautiful son
And sent for a nurse were near.

Away by the water so clear,
They carried the beautiful child.
To his own tender mother his sister and brothers,
Little Moses looked happy and smiled.
His mother so good done all that she
Could, to rear him and teach him with care.

Away by the sea that was red,
The Moses the servant of God
While in his care the sea was divided
As upward he lifted his rod.
The Jews they crossed but the Pharaoh host
Were drowned in water and lost.

Away on mountain so high,
The last one that ever might be.
While in his victories his hope was most glorious.
And he rested over the garden deceased

When his labor deceased he parted in peace,
And rested in the heavens above it

Scarred Hearts: A Song Poem

In my pocket there's a picture
And a curly lock of hair
A yellow rose that's crushed and faded
A treasure each of them with care
Thru the long years I have wandered
Often wishing I was dead
Thinking of her as my angel
And the last words that she said

Chorus
Only scarred hearts know the aching
Of a broken love and dream
Only a broken hearted lover
Knows the sorrow in between

When she took the ring I gave her
Placed it in my hand and cried
Saying "Darling, keep it for me
I will someday be your bride
When the dark clouds have all vanished
And there's nothing in between
I will come back to you darling
There will be no broken dreams"

Chorus
Only scarred hearts know the aching
Of a broken love and dream
Only a broken hearted lover
Knows the sorrow in between

But this evening as the shadows
Gather 'round my cabin door
Her angel face it seems to haunt me
Does she love me any more
Can it be that I have waited
All in vain and emptiness
Can it be her hopes have blighted
Love is crushed within her breast

Chorus
Only scarred hearts know the aching
Of a broken love and dream
Only a broken hearted lover
Knows the sorrow in between

An Aching Heart

Many years ago I wondered
From my home and all my friends
In my heart there was an aching
That I thought somewhere would end

I have been across the oceans
Far upon the mountains tops
I have traveled the wide world over
But this aching has not stopped

Last night I was dreaming
She was standing by my side
But she belonged to another
And will never be my bride

In her eye's I saw the teardrops
As she smiled and walked away
For I know she yet remembered
The love I had for her one day

I awoke and I was crying
For my heart was broke anew
I recalled the quarrel that ended
Everything we'd planned to do

But she told me when we parted
She would never be my bride
But some day up in heaven
She'd be an angel by my side

In my pocket there's her picture
And the size for her ring
In my heart there's an aching
From the memories they now bring

For Your Comfort

All the word that I could say
Would not erase your grief today
But when you know some one cares
And are standing by ready to share
The weight becomes a little lighter
The days begin a little brighter
Because of those along the way
Who, to have felt your grief today
I to have walked this lonely road
I've bore the sorrow from the load
I've shed tears from my heart in grief
Till it seemed there'd never come relief
I've felt the emptiness around my home
The loneliness of just being alone
So dear one words help but can't erase
The sorrow now that you will face
But the sweet words our Savior said
Has comfort for each tear we shed
Thru sorrows valley, day by day

His love knows how to comfort all the way
For he said, I'll never leave thee
Nor forsake thee

Hebrews 13:5

These words came to me, as a song. I'll try to sing it so bare with me as my voice don't hold out so good as it once did.

Yes, I know my blessed Savior cares for me
Or he wouldn't gave his life on Calvary
He would never bare those nails that pierced his hands
If he hadn't had such love for sinful man

He would never carried his cross to Calvary's hill
Where he knew his own life's blood would all be spilled
He would never took the scorn and mock and shame
As he hung upon the cross dying in pain

Chorus

Yes, I know my savior cares for me
Yes, I know he cares for me
All my burdens he will share
Oh yes I know my Savior cares for me

Angels never would have rolled away that stone
If redemptions plan had not been for his own
He would never conquered death and hell and grave
If it hadn't been for sinful man to save

He would not be building mansions up above
If it wasn't for the souls of those he loves
And he'd never come back to this earth again
If it wasn't for the saints that bear his name

Chorus

Yes, I know my savior cares for me
Yes, I know he cares for me
All my burdens he will share
Oh yes I know my Savior cares for me

When Some One Prays

Sing

One day I was discouraged
My heart seemed broke inside
My burden was so heavy
I just sat down and cried

My eyes with tears were blinded
I could not see my way
My words were weak and empty
It seemed I could not pray.

But some where in my pathway
Some one was passing by
They saw that I was burdened
They heard me as I cried.

Then some where in the shadows
I know they called my name
It seemed a hand then touched me
I knew that they were praying

Then a light shone on my pathway
My tears were soon all gone
I felt my burden lifting
In my heart there came this song.

Some one stood at my cross roads
When in my darkest hour
In faith they took my burden
And talked to God in prayer.

Read

Friends, many times the cares of this life
Can become so heavy to bear
And we need to stand at the cross roads
Calling some one's name in prayer.

When we see some one weeping
Lets not just pass them by
But kneel some where in the shadows
Tell God we heard them cry.

In faith lets lift their burdens
Take them to the Lord in prayer
Interceding at their cross roads
To save them from despair.

I think of Gethsemane's garden
Where Jesus often prayed
I think of that great intercessary prayer
Just before he was betrayed.

Perhaps he called your name and mine
When he knelt alone that night
When he carried all our sins and burdens
To pay the price with his own blood and life.

So let's remember his precious words
When he said to pray for one another
Lets stand at some ones cross road
Help lift the burden of a sister or brother.

Given at a Sunday church special.

Alone in Tears

When I left you little darling
In my angry state of mind
I thot my love for you was over
Some one else then I would find

But the years have proved it different
I only find I was to blame
I was angry, cold and jealous
While you've always been the same

Chorus

So I've learned my lesson darling
Just the way you said, my dear
While you're happy, true and smiling
I go on alone in tears

Untitled Work, No Date (2)

*These words came to me, as a song. I'll try to sing it so bare with me
as my voice don't hold out so good as it once did.*

Yes, I know my blessed Savior cares for me
Or he wouldn't gave his life on Calvary
He would never bare those nails that pierced his hands
If he hadn't had such love for sinful man

He would never carried his cross to Calvary's hill
Where he knew his own life's blood would all be spilled
He would never took the scorn and mock and shame
As he hung upon the cross dying in pain

Chorus

Yes, I know my savior cares for me
Yes, I know he cares for me
All my burdens he will share
Oh yes I know my Savior cares for me

Angels never would have rolled away that stone
If redemptions plan had not been for own
He would never conquered death and hell and grave
If it hadn't been for sinful man to save

He would not be building mansions up above
If it wasn't for the souls of those he loves
And he'd never come back to this earth again
If it wasn't for the saints that bear his name

Chorus

Yes, I know my savior cares for me
Yes, I know he cares for me
All my burdens he will share
Oh yes I know my Savior cares for me

Why Not Pray

(Tune - Why Do You Wait)

Sometime my pathway in life
Is shaded and crowded with care
And then I wonder if someone
Is lifting me up in their prayer.

Chorus:
Why not? Why not? Why not pray today?
Why not? Why not? Someone needs you to pray.

Sometimes the trials are many
And burdens so heavy to bear,
My steps grow weak and weary
Have you lifted me up in prayer?

Chorus:
Why not? Why not? Why not pray today?
Why not? Why not? Someone needs you to pray.

There's someone out in the darkness
The Gospel has never heard,
Are we praying for someone to reach them
And tell them of God's holy word?

Chorus:
Why not? Why not? Why not pray today?
Why not? Why not? Someone needs you to pray.

Someone has fell by the wayside
No friends and no one to care,
Will we kneel by the side of our brother
And mention his name in our prayer?

Chorus:
Why not? Why not? Why not pray today?
Why not? Why not? Someone needs you to pray.

Lets weep with those who are weeping
And sing with those who are gay
But remember lets plead for others
Who never have learned to pray.

Chorus:
Why not? Why not? Why not pray today?
Why not? Why not? Someone needs you to pray.

Deanna Wheeler/ Lake Sun

Celebrating 100 years, Wealthy Culvert still plays her favorite hymns on a harmonica she carries with her. Niece Ola Cross says her aunt not only plays the harmonica but, at one time, her mother's violin and sang at church as well.

Wealthy, age 100, with her niece, Ola Cross

Religious

Pathway

One day it seemed my pathway
Was filled with cares and unhappy things
Yet my soul was searching for
The best that life could bring.

When in these trying moments round me
Somewhere near me then I heard
I found there such a sweetness
In the song of a little bird

Then a breeze soft as a whisper
Brushed across my face
And left its cool refreshness
In a quietness every place.

Then I paused in silent meditation
I found another sweetness there
In the embrace of God's presence
That seemed to lift all my cares

In all these things I found life's best
And at the close of my day
I found a happiness in my soul
From Gods sweetness along my way

The Touch of God's Hand

If I had never seen the beauty
In a sunset so far away
I'd never known of God's great artistry
In his touch at the close of day

If I'd never seen the beautiful rainbow
That's often stretched across the sky

I'd never known of that great promise
That God has recorded for you and I

If I had never seen the spring time beauty
Never heard the singing of the birds
I'd never known the beauty of creation
That is recorded in God's holy words

If I'd never known of Gods salvation
Had never shared in his love
I'd never known of his great blessings
That he shares with me from above

If I'd never known his touch of healing
Nor felt the soothe of sorrows pains
I'd never known of God's great comfort
That I see in life's daily picture frames

No I'll never see the lofty mountains
Nor his many creations across the land
But I will see the greatness of his wisdom
In the touch from his hand

Lord Help Me

Lord help me see beauty in a sunset
When the clouds are ugly dark and gray
When I look for its usual loveliness
That I often see at close of day

Help me to see your mighty touch
Across the darkened sky
When there's thunder and lightning flashing
With storm clouds rushing by

Help me to accept the bitterness
If I may suffer in some defeat
Help me then to look to Calvary
Renewed in faith more complete

Help me there to find an answer
An assurance I had never known
A deeper knowledge for my choices
That I must make for my own

Give me friends that I can trust
Someone to pray and hold up my hands
When my cross gets to heavy
And I need more strength to stand

Help me to trust in your promise
Give me wisdom for trying hours
And when I meet with life's ugliness
I'll find beauty in your love and power

August 1983

Life Has Reward

Many times as evening shadows
Closes out the rush of day
I often feel such a loneliness
With the dark night on its way

No footsteps to break the silence
No loved ones in their chair
No voice in conversation
Just a quietness everywhere

But yet in all the stillness
I know I am not alone

For he who is closer than a brother
Never leaves or forsakes his own

For I know in all the quietness
I hear him speak in my soul
And the comfort of his presence
Is more precious than any gold

Sometimes I wish I could see his face
Feel the nail scars in his hands
See my mansion he is building
In that fair and celestial land

Where we could walk and talk together
And with my loved ones meet
See no faces stained with tears
As we walk those golden streets

No lonely nights with its darkness
But in the brightness of his love
In that home of God's eternal victory
With his redeemed in Heaven above

Walking together in beautiful gardens
Where flowers are all in bloom
Breathe the air that's pure and laden
With the sweetness of their perfume

Yes, exploring Heaven will never end
New adventures every day
No night no curse heartaches of pain
To mar our happiness in any way

God's love will never cease unfolding
New life with the redeemed

The greatness of a new heaven and earth
Ear has not heard, nor eye has seen

Yes, this is the place I want to explore
Not in flights prepared by man
But in the home coming of my soul
Launched by Gods sovereign hand

If God is Dead

If God is dead, who puts the rainbow in the sky,
Who paints the sunset at close of the day?
Who gives the calm that stills the tempest
In life's storms along the way?

If God is dead, who holds the stars in their place?
Who teaches the little birds to sing?
Who makes the changes in the season?
Renew the earth, seed time and harvest in everything?

If God is dead, who soothes, when our hearts are broken?
Who gives us strength, hope and faith each day,
Whose voice is it, we hear in our soul,
Answering prayers that we pray?

If God is dead, who sets a baby's heart in motion?
Who makes it breathe with life within,
Who holds the number of its days,
Who designed for its life to begin?

If God is dead, who puts the beauty in the lilies,
Who puts the fragrance in the rose?
Who gives new life in the springtime,
To earth that was dormant, bare and froze?

Life is full of proof and warmness,
Sacred, rich, pure and divine,
He is not dead, He's alive,
This God of mine.

God is in the Sunset

I stood by my window this evening,
Looking far into the west
Where there was a beautiful sunset
All arrayed in its best.

All seemed so quiet and peaceful
In this beauty so far a way
As if I lived in another world
In a dawn of another day.

I felt the love he has for me
Saw the holiness in all its splendor
Heard his voice speak in my soul.
From the beauty seen from my window.

In these moments I got a glimpse
Of the masters nail scarred hand
I felt anew the sweet assurance
I felt his great redemption plan.

I saw a new depth in sovereign power
Greater security in the divine
I said "Oh God how great your love
To let me be a child of thine."

To let me look out from my window
And in a beautiful sunset there
See your hand, hear your voice
And know you are with me everywhere.

Our God is Not Dead

When thunder roars through clouds over head
And lightnings play around our feet
All creation clutched in his mighty power
Humanity stands by helpless and in defeat

When mighty winds lay waste and destruction
Across the world in every land
When floods break all barriers with gushing fury
Humanity in defeat and helpless stand

When mighty quakes play underneath
The earth seems to lose all holds
Trembling, reeling and sinking
Gulping cities beneath its folds

Man in weakness stands in awe
Where cometh such mighty power?
Who holds our life in embrace
In such a tragic hour?

Who dares to say that God is dead
Who restores in our defeats?
What hand holds this earth he made
When it reels and trembles under our feet

Who dares to say that God is dead
Who can stay his mighty hand?
Who can spurn his mighty love
Even when we don't understand?

Who dares to say that God is dead
He gives us hope in life's storms
His unfailing love hides our soul
In greater faith as we press on.

In Him, I See

Lord, help me to see the beauty
In your pretty flowers that grow,
Help me breathe their sweet fragrance
When the gentle breezes blow.

Let me hear 'round about me,
The songs you gave to birds.
Perhaps in praise to their maker
In a language we've never heard.

Let me see through the rain drops
In a warm summer shower
The untouchable colors in the rainbow
God's promise, in beauty, love, and power.

Let me see a beauty in the sunsets
Thru the clouds when dark and gray,
Let me see the touch of the master
Who colored them his way.

When I need a strength and comfort
Someone, my burdens share
Let me find a Gethsemane garden
And take them to the lord in prayer.

There let me find the assurance
In the sweetness of God's love
Where I can feel his holy spirit
In a sacred touch from above.

God's Promises

Some day there will be a happy gathering
Time of this life will not be remembered

Of the sad hours and tears I have shed
For things I loved for friends and family members

In this new life there will be no more sorrows
No partings or cause for tears
What a glorious dawning that will be
In eternities unnumbered years

There will be no more stains of sin
No place for partings, no cause for tears
No memories of heartaches or worries
No more crying, no more fears

But in that sacredness of eternal happiness
That we have never known
We will enter that new life in eternity
That god has prepared for his own

So let me not be questioning
When I have to wipe away my tears
Knowing there awaits a comfort
In God's eternity of unending years

June 30, 1996

Exploring Heaven

Sometimes I stand gazing up as far as I can see
But no other planets I want to explore
The only place I long to search out
Is God's eternal blissful shore

There to meet my savior first of all
My Lord who gave his life for me
To see his hands scared by the nails
That kept him hanging on Calvary's tree

I want to feel the touch of those hands
As he wipes away all my tears
Feel his embrace of eternal life
With no more pain, grief, or fears

I want to see the mansions he has prepared
For me to call my very own
See its great designed beauty
Not made with hands in that home

I want to touch the tree of life
Drink from the river pure and clear
I want t listen to Heaven's choir
See the glory of God everywhere

I want to meet with loved ones I've missed so long
Mother and dad for long I've cried
I want to join with my companion
Exploring Heaven side by side

Untitled Work, No Date (3)

(Sing)
He is not here, but he is risen
The tomb is empty where he lay
Go your way, tell the Disciples
You will meet him on your way

(Read)

I gaze down in the empty tomb
Where once my Lord did lay
Where death and hell could not hold him
Immortality could not stay

I see the blood as they pierced his side
No death was in its flow
Only cleansing healing power
Warm with life did it glow

I see the price that he paid
To redeem the soul of man
I see a love that conquered all
In his great redemption plan

I see the stone that was rolled away
I hear the angels say
He is not here, but he is risen
You'll meet him on the way

And as I see the son of God
In full triumphed power
And as I see him in eternal life
I look beyond Calvary's hour

I look beyond his empty tomb
Beyond his death and pain
I look upon my risen Lord
The hope of life again

I know I too shall live again
The clutch of death was broke
In that first resurrection morning
When the angel spoke

He is not here, but he is risen
See the place where he laid
Go your way, tell the disciples
And be not afraid

And when that great resurrection morning
Dawns for his own
Won't that be a glad reunion
With the loved ones we have known

Beauty in the Master's Touch

Today I stood looking out my window
The sun was just going down
Its rays were hid by darkened clouds
All was gray, ugly, everywhere around

I wondered where was all the beauty
I often see in sun sets fair
But now just a bank of ugliness
With evening shadows everywhere

As I watched this changing ugliness
In this sunset so far away
I tried to find some where a beauty
To curtain off another day

Then I saw a touch of the Master's hand
These words came shining thru
"He who put the colors in the rainbow
Put the colors in the sunset to"

Yes, I saw a beauty then unfolding
From my window I walked away
I had found a loveliness in the sunset
Where my Master's hand touched today.

The Power of Prayer

I came to a mountain in my path one day
Before me it stood like a great stone wall

I could not climb it, it was high and wide
No way to cross it or pass it at all

I stood and looked and wondered just how
Such a barrier before me could ever be moved
The mission I was on was for the Lord
And no turning back and this I knew

I saw the helplessness in my self
I felt the weakness in my power
My strength alone could never be proved
To meet my need for such an hour

But in my despair there was a faith within
That held before me a flaming key
I knew all the barriers it could unlock
That stood like giants facing me

I saw the nail scarred hand before me
Thru these scars I saw a light
A path had parted in the mountains
There was victory in sight

Satan places many barriers around us
Mountains he thinks we cannot cross
But with a faith that holds the key to prayer
He meets defeat and suffers loss

God Has a Place for Me

Many times I've wished I had the voice
To sing like folks I have heard
Or could play like some do in music
Or preach like some do from God's word

Perhaps there are some very good reasons
Just why I cannot do these things
Maybe because I never had the training
Or results that practice brings

But I think of that great true story
In the Bible where I've read
Of the two little fishes
And the five loaves of bread

How Jesus fed five thousand people
Who were hungry when they came
They all did eat and where filled
And twelve baskets of food remained

From this story I have learned
More about God's sufficient grace
And in my soul I hear him say
There's no one else who can fill your place

Perhaps God made a place for me
At the foot of Calvary's cross
Where I can kneel in its shadow
Intercede for someone that's lost

But whatever talent he has placed
In my hands for me to hold
May they be used for his glory
To bring him, five or ten, or a hundred fold

And when I awake some brighter morn
And on some fairer shore
With Jesus by my side I'll learn
The things I did not know

My Souls Reward

When this my soul that God once gave me
For these many years that I have known
I know there's coming a departure
It will return to God as his own

But in that great resurrection morning
His promises I will gain
My soul will be restored a new
And in a new body, I will live again

In that eternity that God has promised
For those who are called by his name
When the earth has become all new
Only life with eternal happiness will remain

No more sin, sickness or death
Only God's everlasting holiness will be known
As he walks and talks together
With the redeemed that are his own

What a blessed eternity that will be
Eye hath not seen, nor ear hath heard
For those, whose soul has been chosen
For their acceptance and obedience in his Holy word

Revelation Chapter 21 and 22

March 1996

My Testimony

Beyond the sunset of this life
Where eternal day dawns for me

With the brightness of Heaven's glory
A beauty I have longed to see

My thoughts in sweet inspirations
That I've received so many times
I'll be given complete understanding
Of their wisdom to my mind

There I'll live in a perfect knowledge
Thru obedience I have gained
By listening when my Lord was speaking
And calling me by name

Not questioning when all around me
Many times was dark, I stood alone
But in the hour of every testing
I learned he cared for his own

And in patience I accepted
Whatever the cross to be mine
With the touch of an unseen hand
I knew my way I could find

Thru the scars of the unseen hand
There was a light shining through
A voice spoke in sweet assurance
"I will never leave, nor forsake you"

When my days work on earth have ended
Beyond the shadows of the night
I'll gain the victory he has promised
In a land so pure and bright

What a joy for me is waiting
When eternal dawn I can see

To gain the beauty of Heaven's inspiration
As I listen to Jesus talk to me

Thy Will Be Done

Let me use these hands of mine
To gather sheaves and them to bind
Touch not things that are unclean
But scatter seeds of beautiful things

Reach out to those who are in need
Lift up the fallen who are weak
Let me use these feet of mine
To bear me over the paths of time

Where I may reach a traveling one
Lost in despair, their hopes undone
That I may share a word of cheer
As did my Lord when he was here

Let me use this voice he gave
To say kind words and sing and pray
To lift above a world of strife
A ray of hope, a Christian light

To tell the world of one who died
Upon the cross was crucified
He to redeem all lost mankind
Through his blood in faith divine

Oh let my words be ever true
And let my steps be ever sure
And let my life always portray
The love of Christ each night and day

For there are those who tread alone
Hungering for some light to come
Waiting for a helping hand
To Guide them o're life's sinking sands

Let me live this life of mine
Centered in his will divine
Submissive in his hands I pray
Binding sheaves along the way

January 1943

Alone with Jesus

When evening shade begin to fall
At the closing of the day
I feel such a loneliness in words
I could not say

I think of other days gone by
With vacant chairs around
When there were those near and dear
Voices and footstep sounds

When I planned for tomorrow
With work that needed done
It seemed such a pleasure
When a new day had begun

With someone to advise in problems
Or help carry some heavy load
Plan and work together
To smooth life's roughest road

But times have changed thru many years
Yet on the screen of my mind

I review the many memories
Those happier days of mine

One by one footsteps grew silent
Voices ceased of those I loved to hear
Vacant chairs now look so empty
Loneliness comes with many tears

One by One, God has called away
Those who made my happy home
But with faith in his great promise
I know he is with me, I am not alone

Someday when my earthly span of life
Ceases to be no more
I'll wake in the eternal morning
Join with loved ones forever more.

God's Garden

God has planted another rose
In his garden up above
To bloom for another soul
He called home one he loved

In a paradise so sweet
Where eyes cannot behold
And words cannot describe
Such beauty we are told

Where the air is pure and fragrant
With God's love every day
With Angels walking in the sweetness
Where my mother has gone to stay

Where she sees the face of Jesus
And can hear his gentle voice
And is happy in his presence
Because she made him her choice

While I must stay here a little longer
Finish work that I must do
Let me keep my eyes toward Heaven
With a faith steadfast and true

Walk my journey to its ending
Till my mission along the way
Brave the storms of life alone
Till someday I'll hear him say

My child it's time for you to come
To your garden up above
Another rose has been planted
For your soul that I love

Then together with my loved ones
Where years will never end
Throughout God's eternal ages
We'll live and love together again.

Wealthy in her garden at her home near Montreal, Missouri

Take Your Brother by the Hand

Take your brother by the hand
Lift him up and help him stand
When you see his feet are sinking down
Beneath a slippery, miry ground.

Perhaps some trial has been too hard
And his faith has been marred
Perhaps his strength gave away too soon
And he felt despair was his doom.

Maybe a friend along the way
Was untrue and him betrayed
Maybe someone failed to lift his load
When he stood at life's crossroads.

We never know lots of times
The cause of things in people's minds
We cannot see the path they tread
Or know the things they have to dread.

Many times their souls are starved
For the things that has been barred
Perhaps, because, maybe you and I
Was just a friend that passed on by.

Maybe just a clasp of the hand
From someone else who understands
Maybe just a sail would pave his way
And start his steps toward a brighter day.

For those who are neath life's heavy clouds
Within themselves cry aloud
They grasp the faintest ray of light
Oft the first they see in sight.

So take your brother by the hand
Lift him up and help him stand
Let him see in you the Christ
Who lived and died and paid the price

Take your brother by the hand
When he steps in sinking sand
Let Heaven's light direct his way
Because you signaled at the crossroads today.

February 1933

<u>*A Mansion Awaiting*</u>

St. John 14:2-3

I often think of Heaven
And all the joys sublime,
Yet sometimes I hardly realize
That a mansion there is mine.
When I think of my little being,
And so little I have done,
And so little I have given,
And so little I have won.

But the soul that's been perfected
In the blood of the lamb,
Becomes an heir in God's glory
And a child of his I am.
His gentle voice that speaks to all
One day said, "Follow me";
I heeded and was born again,
And now in Him I'm free.

As we walk and talk together,
Through the days that come and go

His tender love never changes,
My faith more steadfast grows.
For I know in Him is perfection,
All that's pure and divine,
Where I'll live the aspirations
Of this soul of mine.

In a mansion that is waiting
When I cross to the other side,
Where I'll drop this flesh and weakness
In death's swollen tide.
In his likeness I will emerge,
Breath eternal life,
Join in singing perfect praises
With my Savior's face in sight.

That Beautiful Place

1 Corinthians 2:9

There'll be no sorrow in Heaven,
For the Bible tells me so,
No more heartaches, trials or trouble
It's a place of ended woe.

There'll be no enemies up there
All will be quiet with love,
Happy and singing with the angels,
In a home of peace above.

The back biters won't be there,
With their poisonous tongues and lies,
No evil thoughts will be up there
In that home up in the skies.

None of the filthy things of earth,
Will reach that fair land
None but the pure in heart,
Shall join the Heavenly band.

All the hatred, greed and grudges,
That keep folks in a fight,
Those things won't reach Heaven,
They can't bear the beautiful light.

None but the pure in heart
In that fair land shall stand,
Only those who have been washed
In the blood of the lamb.

What a beautiful place just beyond
This world of many cares,
And God has given us the privilege,
This beautiful place to share.

By Our Fruits We are Known

Matthew 7:20

The other day I stopped beside a tree
With grape vines twining there.
The grapes were hanging thickly,
But My! They were so sour.

I picked a bunch as usual,
But soon threw them down.
They were just to sour to eat,
Without a dozen frowns.

The birds and had gone and left them,
Of sweeter things they knew.

I surely did not blame them,
For I passed on by them too.

But they spoke a lesson to me.
"By our fruits we are known",
And we gather in the harvest,
From the seeds that are sown.

Some time our life as human beings,
Is far too sour indeed.
When all around about us,
Are hearts that ache and bleed.

Who needs the touch of a helping hand,
Kind words that we could say.
Or just a smile sometime can drive,
The darkest gloom away.

In a world that is sick and saddened,
Can we be more thoughtful and kind.
Can we stand by as a friend and neighbor.
Be sweet fruit that they can find.

The Narrow Way

I have found that narrow pathway thru life,
The one that Jesus trod
And I'm so happy, secure and at peace
For I know it leads to God.

Old Satan gets mad and he sneers and laughs,
He tries to tell me his lies,
He calls me old fashioned and mocks in my face,
When praying I would try.

Some time he tempts me so boldly and sly,
He wants to be sure of me,
But the salvation I got at the foot of the cross,
Is what that keeps me free.

For I know he tempted my Savior to,
Be he said, "Satan get thee behind,"
And in this narrow pathway of life,
His tracks I never could find.

And as older I grow, and brave the trials
And hold to my Savior's hand,
Each testing just proves that he is true,
His power abroad in our land.

And as I journey, a stranger while here,
God is acquainted with me
And I'm not ashamed of the old fashion way
For it's the Jesus led way for me.

That's why I've fell out with the folly of the world
I never find Jesus there,
His footsteps lead straight on ahead
Where I find him kneeled in prayer

And if I must depend on service from him,
I must call where he abides,
And if he has something to say to me,
I must be on the connected line.

So friends please choose the narrow way
The journey won't be so long
It'll all grow sweeter at the end of the way
When we hear the angels songs.

We'll forget the trials and heartaches here
When we see him face to face.
When we join in praise with the redeemed
Who've won thru life's hard race.

1940

Precious Things

Life has so many precious things.
Little children in their happy play
Youth with its love, hopes and dreams,
A future promise for every day.

The evening beauty in a sunset
In a rainbow arched overhead,
The silence in which she labors,
As a timid spider spins her web.

Birds singing in the woodlands
Flowers that bloom after winter's blight
With a fragrance to scent the breezes
Twinkling stars overhead at night.

On and on but words could never number
The precious things that God has made
Sweet fellowship in communion
In prayers that are prayed

But his great crowning beauty is in
His precious love for all mankind
When he gave his son to die on a cross
Shed his blood for your sins and mine

He Has Promised

When my pathway leads thru valleys
With dark clouds overhead
I am glad there's a lily blooming
With sweet fragrance 'round me spread

I am glad there's a bright star shining
Far above my stormy way
A ray of light penetrating
To guide and comfort me each day

Tho' I may grow tired and weary
Yet, in my soul I can sing,
For I can feel a renewing
In strength like eagle wings.

Hear him say, "I'm that lily in your valley
I'm that star that's shining bright
My nail scarred hand is guiding you,
Thru every fear and darkened night.

So with this promise I feel assured
In my helplessness I won't be alone,
Beside me an ever blooming lily
And a light in all my paths unknown

1984

God is Everywhere

Today I stood looking some roses
That were just fresh in bloom
Such beauty that I saw in them
And smelled such sweet perfume.

It seemed I could even see
A smile among the petals fair
Hear whispers in nature's language
They knew I was standing there

A softened breeze a silken touch
A glint of morning sun
The dew then from them vanished
Their day had just begun

Nodding, unfolding and smiling
In their beauty and fragrant way
I saw and felt a touch of God
It was his voice I heard today

I said yes, God I see your beauty
Your love I've learned to know
I'm glad I find you everywhere,
Even in the heart of a rose.

God's Sweetness

One day it seemed my pathway
Was full of cares and unhappy things
Yet my soul was searching for
The best that life could bring

But in these trying moments 'round me
Some where near me then I heard
And there I found such a sweetness
In the song of a little bird

I found then another sweetness
From the flower that was in bloom
That grew along my pathway
And shared with me their rare perfume

Then a breeze, soft as a whisper
Brushed across my face
And left it's cool refreshness
In a quietness, every place

Then I paused in silent meditation
I found another sweetness there
In the embrace of God's presence
That seemed to lift all my cares

In all these things, I found life's best
And at the close of my day
I found a happiness in my soul
From God's sweetness along my way.

Thorns in the Flesh

It seems there are many Christians
That has a thorn in their flesh
Because sometimes along their way
Their faith weakened by an unfair test.

Satan watches for these moments
And he quickly draws a line
To place in their conscience
A failure to keep in their mind.

He does not want us to remember
When Jesus once wrote on the ground
When sinful men brought that innocent woman
But no sin in her could be found

What did Jesus say to them
Did he accept what they told
Did he lay this sinful accusation
To the life of an innocent soul

We do not know what he wrote
With his finger on the ground
But I believe what it could have been
Mercy calls and justice will be found

We know Jesus said to her accusers
"You with out sin cast the first stone"
And they in their guilty conscience fled
With Jesus the innocent woman stood alone

But perhaps thru her remaining life
That accusation left a stain
That she once had been accused
That brought disgrace to her name

Paul had a thorn in his flesh
What it was no one has ever known
Perhaps because of some false accusation
With no one worthy to cast a stone

Perhaps in lives of many people
Whose hearts feel the sting
From the thorn of false accusation
That injustice always brings

But let us always remember
When Jesus wrote on the ground
And said to her accuser
No sin in this woman can be found

March 1992

He Hath Promised

As I go thru darkened valleys
Where no sun ever shines

I find my way thru darkness
With my Saviors hand in mine.

When my heart is gripped in sorrow
And briny tears from its depths
Overflow from my eyes
And drop in my steps.

Its then I find his words most precious
"I'll never leave nor forsake"
"Cast all your cares upon me"
I have balm for hearts that break.

When those I love prove unfaithful
And my trust in them is vain
And my conscience then seems served
From a love that causes pain.

Its then in Jesus I find complete a trust
I have in no other
When again from his words I hear
He sticketh closer than a brother.

Thru all of life's uneven journey
Let me reap in the narrow way
Ne'er losing sight of the master's footsteps
Nor things that he did say.

Striving forward for perfection
Where the souls of God's redeemed
Shall know the joy of heaven's beauty
Where the angels forever sing.

Faith Has Reward

When death must close its door to me
To a world of sorrow pain and sin
My soul will enter its Heaven reward
That I have gained thru faith in him

Life's many battles that I have fought
The many tears I've had to shed
Discouragements I've met along the way
The many storms I've had to dread

Many times my path was hard to find
Across hills so high and steep
Thru valleys so dark and narrow
When my strength seemed so weak

Many times I've gave way to self
I was prone to question why
But thru faith's unseen touch
A sustaining power was always nigh

In these hours of human weakness
My soul was bowed within
With a faith my Savior sealed
When I gave my life to him

Satan's moments in Eden's garden
That cursed the human race
God yet loved his creation
Retained in man, his power of faith

His love so great, so sure and rich
His plan could not be lost
Redemption for man must be paid
Thru death of his son on a rugged cross

That power of faith he retained for man
Thru cleansing blood of his son
To give us hope and strength and promise
Till our work on earth is done

Then in victory from the curse of Satan
When death to man he did bring
We'll know the love and power in God's redemption
Oh grave where is your victory and death where is thy sting

1st Corinthians 15:55

Testimony I gave one nite in a revival at Buffalo Prairie
Church. November 24, 1928, I gave my life to the Lord in a
revival here at Buffalo Prairie. Almost 58 years ago. Thru the
years with all the ups and downs I have never doubted my
experience of salvation. During my acquaintance with my
Lord and Savior I have had many precious experiences of his
love and power in fellowship with him. As I draw nearer to
the end of my life's journey my great desire is to meet my
Lord face to face, feel his tender embrace and touch of his nail
scared hands.

Play on Harp

Blessed assurance, Jesus is mine
Oh what a foretaste of glory divine
Heir of salvation, purchase of God
Born of his spirit, washed in his blood
This is my story, this is my song
Praising my Savior, all the day long
This in my story, this is my song
Praising my Savior, all the day long

Alone With Jesus

When evening shades begin to fall,
At the closing of the day,
I feel such a loneliness,
In words I could not say.

I think of other days gone by,
With no vacant chairs around,
When there were those near and dear,
Voices and foot step sounds

When I planned for tomorrow,
With work that needed done,
It seemed such a pleasure,
When a new day had begun.

With some one to advise in problems,
Or help carry some heavy load,
Plan and work together,
To smooth life's roughest road.

But times have changed thru many years,
Yet on the screen of my mind,
I review thru my memories,
those happier days of mine.

One by one foot steps grew silent,
Voices ceased that I loved to hear,
Vacant chairs look so empty,
Loneliness comes with many tears.

One by one, God called away,
Those who made my happy home,
But with faith in his great promise,
I know he'll be with me, I'm not alone.

And some day when my earthly span of life,
Will cease to be no more,
I'll awake in that eternal morning,
Join with my loved ones forever more.

March 26, 1984

<u>*He is Risen*</u>

Yes, know my blessed Savior cares for me.

As I look away to that empty tomb
Where once my Lord did lay
Where death and Hell could not hold him
Immortality could not stay

I see the blood as they pierced his side
No death was in its flow
Only cleansing healing power
Warm with life it did glow

I see the price that paid
To redeem the soul of man
I see a love that conquered all
In his great redemption plan

I see the stone that was rolled away
I hear the angels say
He is not here, he is risen
You'll meet him on the way

And as I see the son of God
In full triumphant power
And as I see him in eternal life
I look beyond Calvary's hour

I look beyond his empty tomb
Beyond his death and pain
I look upon him as my risen Lord
The hope of life again

For I know I to shall live again
The clutch of death was broke
In that first resurrection morning
When these words, the angels spoke

He is not here, he is risen
See the place where he laid?
Go your way tell the disciples
And be not afraid

And in that great resurrection morning
When he comes for his own
Won't that be a great reunion
When God's children all get home

Love

An Old Love

I sit here alone tonight my darling
Thinking how happy you must be
With some one's arms around you
With a love so sweet and free

But I have no one to blame my darling
In my heart I knew I lied
When I told you I did not love you
So choose another for your bride

You took me at my word and left me
Now another wears your name
And I can only see the happiness
I missed by being to blame

When I see your ring around her finger
See the smile upon her face
See the happiness you have given her
I know she only fills my place

And as I pass you by on the street
I yet feel a burning flame
From the love you once had for me
Tho' another now wears your name

Your Words Were Daggers in my Heart

You just seemed to want to hurt me
And that's just what you have done
You placed a dagger in my heart
With poison from your tongue

Something told me when we met dear
That your love would be untrue

But I did not heed the warning
I just kept on loving you

You was jealous and deceitful
And your love all fell apart
And your words were only daggers
Filled with poison from the start

Now my heart is torn and bleeding
And that's just what you have done
Your words were only daggers
With poison from your tongue

Now you've gone away and left me
With a past I can't forget
With my heart all torn and bleeding
Filled with daggers of regret

My Heart is Detoured for Repair

Just stay away, keep out of sight
That thing called love has broke my heart
That detour signs for you to see
For it was you who tore it all apart

My heart is detoured for repair
It's cold and hard as it can be
Just stay away, keep out of sight
For it was you who made a wreck of me

I always let you have your way
I thot your love was always fair
But your game was just to crush and break
And make my heart be detoured for repair

Just stay away, keep out of sight
My life will never be the same
That thing called love has broke my heart
That detour sign will always bear my name

November 29, 1956

<u>*A True, But Broken Heart*</u>

In sending you this package
I'm sending it to you by air
It's my heart that you have broken
Mind you handle it with care

You broke this heart when you told me
That you threw my ring away
You said your love for me was over
And you meant what you did say

But remember little darling
To my dreams this is the end
But someday you'll learn the truth dear
It was caused by jealous friends

So that's the reason I am sending
You a true but broken heart
Time will prove that you could trust me
After we are far apart

<u>*A Broken Love*</u>

In my pocket there's a picture
And a curly lock of hair
A rose bud crushed and faded
Each I treasure with care

Thru the long years I have wondered
Often wishing I was dead
Thinking of her as my angel
And the last words that she said

Tho, only scarred hearts know the aching
Of a broken love and dream
Only a broken hearted lover
Knows the sorrow in between

When she took the ring I gave her
Placed it in my hand and cried
Saying, Darling keep it for me,
I will some day be your bride

When the dark clouds all have vanished
And there's nothing in between
I will come back to you darling
They'll be no broken dreams

Tho, only broken hearts know the aching
Of a broken love and dream
Only a broken hearted lover
Knows the sorrow in between

But this evening as the shadows
Gather round my cabin door
Her face is seemed to haunt me
Does she love me any more

Can It be that I have waited
All in vain and emptiness
Can it be her hopes have blighted
Love is crushed with her breast

I Don't Cry Over You

I don't cry over you any more
For you told me my love we were thru
No more tears do I shed, no wet pillows on my bed
For I don't cry over you

I don't cry over you any more
I can find some one else who is true
Now my heart does not ache , no more nights to lay awake
For I don't cry over you

All my dreams will come true by and by
No use wasting my tears over you
I'll be happy again in my heart be no more pain
For I don't cry over you

The Newly Weds

Surely God in his great wisdom
Has placed his hand upon your life
And it has been of his own choosing
For you to become as man and wife

So as you start this journey together
Hand in hand and side by side
You may find hills steep to climb
And valleys that are dark and wide

Storm clouds will gather now and then
The sky will not show thru
The sun will hide its face at times
Dark clouds will cover you

But as you share your life together
Love will bridge the gaps between

His hand will lead thru uncertain places
On his arm you can lean

He has crossed thru all your shadows
He has seen every tear
He will hear all your footsteps
And you will know that he is near

As you join your faith together
May it arch and bridge your way
Then the love that he has chosen
Will be enriched and blessed each day.

1994

<u>*Congratulations*</u>

There's nothing sweeter than loves young dreams
When there seems no problems and nothing to mar.
When the future looks wreathed in happy days,
With nothing to cause a hurtful scar.

But as you travel your journey together,
There'll be many hills for you to climb,
Many valleys you will have to cross,
Bitter tears to shed many times.

Your lives will never be free from all,
The thorns along the way.
But you will learn to walk among them,
Holding hands day by day.

The sun will often hide its face,
Dark clouds will come between.
Your plans will sometimes be shattered,
And lessen all your dreams.

But as you share your joys and griefs together,
Let faith arch and bridge your way.
Let your love that God has chosen,
Be enriched and blessed each day.

And when the years have come and gone,
Thru victories that you have gained,
You'll continue to see Gods love unfolding,
And loves young dreams won't be in vain.

Holidays

My Easter Vision, 1992

Today I let my faith look yonder
To Calvary's hill where I can see
My Lord dying on a rugged cross
To pay sin's debt for you and me

It seems I feel the painful hurts
From the nails drove in his hands
From the thorns that pierced and poisoned
The brow of the dying son of man

The cruel lashed upon his body
Such pain in the torn flesh
Only Satan could look on in pleasure
And see him dying in such distress

My heart feels the hurts he bore
As he was scorned and mocked in shame
Knowing the innocent son of God
Was guiltless and without blame

But in each pain was sacrifice
His life he was freely giving
There was a victory to be gained
Salvation for sins to be forgiven

But I look away from Calvary's hill
Where I see an empty grave
Where earthly power could not hold him
Immortality could not stay

Death, hell, and the grave had been conquered
The atonement had been made
Salvation's plan is now complete
For all mankind to be saved

When the seal on the tomb was broken
And the great stone rolled away
Resurrection and eternal life came forth
When Jesus walked alive from his grave

So those who were there waiting
To them I hear the angels say
He is not here he has risen
Come see the place where he lay

But go quickly and tell his disciples
That he is risen from the dead
And goeth forth in to Galilee
Alive again, just as he said

Have we met this risen Savior
Somewhere along our way
So we rejoice in that salvation
That he gave his life, sin's debt to pay

1992

My Easter Vision, 1993

This Easter morning I find a great consolation
In a sunrise so far away
Thru eyes of faith I see the sepulcher
Now empty where once my lord did lay

Just the angels are standing there
In garments shining bright
The stone that sealed the tomb
Has been rolled out of sight

All is in a sacred quietness
All around that empty place

Yet a fear grips the hearts
Of those who came to seek his face

The plan of God had been released
And in this silent hour
Death, hell, and the grave were conquered
By God's love and mighty power

I see the blood from those wounds
Warm with love and saving grace
I see God's plan for salvation
His son dying in our place

I see the price that he paid
To redeem the soul of man
I see God's love that conquered sin
In his great redemption plan

Thru faith I view that empty tomb
Seems I hear the angels say
He is not here he is risen
You will meet him on your way

Today that empty tomb has meaning
Where a victory has been won
Salvations plan was made complete
Sins debt was paid for every one

In the power of God's resurrection
The clutch of sin was torn
The gift of life for our soul redemption
Was not sealed by the stone

"Play harp"
I see Jesus, I see Jesus
I see Jesus dying on the cross

I see Jesus dying and bleeding
I see Jesus dying for the lost

Blest be the tie that binds
Our hearts in Christian love
The fellowship of kindred minds
Is like to that above

Thanksgiving

Another season has left the footprints on the pages of time,
Another harvest has been reaped,
God has been good to us, a nation,
Our store houses with plenty is heaped.

Freedom has been ours to enjoy without fear,
No battles fought on our soil,
Our cities and factories and farms and homes,
Where men and women toil,

From all the harvest there's some to give,
To others who are hungry and cold,
From the great, loving hearts of people who care,
To these they will bestow.

Let us pray that our friendship will grip the world,
In a love that is divine,
A faith that will hoist to a darkened world,
God's eternal light to mankind.

ABC Christmas Song

A – is for the Angels that sang long years ago

B – is for the Bible that tells us it is so

C – is for the Christ child in Bethlehem was born

D – is for the day break upon that early morn

E – is for the enemy that sought the baby's life

F – is for the freedom into that Egypt flight

G – is for the gifts that wise men brought to him

H – is for the Heavenly host that sweetly sang to them

I – is for Israel that waited for so long to see the Messiah and hear the Angels song

J – is for Joseph that cared for him so good

K – is for the King that would have killed him if he could

L – is for the light that everyone might see

M – is for the message he brought to you and me

N – is for the nations with sinners great and small

O – is for oppression he came to lift for all

P – is for pardon for those who believe

Q – is for questions he answers for you and me

R – is for redeemer for truly we can say

S – is for sins he takes them all away

T – is for truth he left for all mankind

U – is for union in love and faith divine

V – is for vision we have for lost souls

W – is for work to win them to the fold

X – is for the cross roads in every sinners life

Y – is for you to start your steps aright

Z – is for zeal we put forth every day to win the world for
Jesus when he comes back again some day

A Hobo's Christmas

Down the dusty roads thru summer,
Sleeping under stars and sky,
Asking for food when he was hungry,
Just a hobo passing by.

Living here and there in winter,
No home, no one to care,
No friendly voice to cheer him,
No happy home to share.

No one knew his own life's story,
No one knew his heart was sad,
No one could see the inward scars,
From misfortunes that he'd had.

But his manly pride was to great,
To be trampled under foot,
So from the eyes of the world,
A hobo's life he took.

No one would know his bearded face,
Dark glasses hid his eyes,
And to the world he only meant,
A hobo passing by.

He'd always stood for life's better things,
Till crushed by friends and fate,
And the load was just too heavy,
He fell beneath its weight.

Leaving behind all he loved,
He started another life,
He became another person,
A hobo in disguise.

One night while walking 'long his way,
Singing, reached his ears,
It came from a little church,
That he was coming near.

He slipped up to the window,
The room was large and bright,
Everywhere was trimmed for Christmas,
For it was on Christmas night.

A beautiful tree was in one corner,
Old Santa was looking on,
The preacher held his bible,
The people sang a song.

Gifts were laid underneath the tree,
Wrapped and tied so fine,
Everybody seemed so happy,
At this Christmas time.

Tears started down his face,
He dropped to his knees,
In his heart he cried, "Oh God,
Is there a Christmas for me?"

The people inside started singing,
That dear old familiar hymn,
The one he'd heard his mother sing,
"Oh, Little Town of Bethlehem".

Just then a light shone in his heart,
He heard the angels sing,
"To you a Savior has been born,
Glad tidings to you bring."

He quickly rose to his feet,
He'd felt life's burden lift,
Into his heart the Savior was born,
Gods own Christmas gift.

He left the little church that night,
With joy he did cry,
"The spirit of Christmas fills my soul,
I am God's hobo, passing by."

A Prisoner's Story

Behind these lonely prison walls
My life is being spent
For a crime I did not do
And a sentence I could not prevent

Dishonest friends and unfair judge
Cut me thru like a knife
When the verdict termed me guilty
And sent me here for all my life

All my plans for my future
Were blighted over night
My heart felt like a mass of stone
I could not see a ray of light

A taste of gall seemed in my mouth
Not guilty, but yet condemned
Despised and rejected
By friends and laws of men

Time drew on, this cloud of darkness
Shut the world from my eyes
I was dazed under the weight
Of shame, remorse and lies

One night things became brighter
It was on Christmas Eve
I heard someone ask the warden
If they could come and sing with me

And when I saw their smiling faces
My heart leaped with joy
There stood my own little family
My wife and little boy

Each one held up so bravely
Their face was all aglow
I knew my family loved me
The truth they did know

They began to sing the songs I loved
I joined them once again
We turned our faces toward Heaven
I forgot all the shame

Then I seemed to see the Bible
Lifted fare above the night
And on its open pages there
Shone a clear and radiant light

There the message of salvation
In all its power was unfurled
The glorious gospel for peace of earth
To a dying sinful world

A message of love to every nation
Hope throughout the land
Best for the weary hearted
"Peace on earth, good will toward man"

Then I thought back thru the years
When I was just a boy
How this Jesus saved my soul
And filled my heart with joy

The a voice spoken to my heart
Said "Son I've never turned you down
Although behind these prison walls
With man, you are guilty found"

"Remember, son I'm keeping record
My eyes have searched the land
Vengeance is mine, I will repay
I know the heart of every man"

"Remember, I was once condemned
They hung me on the cross
When I gave my life for sinful men
Made redemption for the lost"

"Shed my blood that it might cleanse
All the sin from every land
Bringing peace to every heart
And good will to every man"

"Yet men go on rejecting me
They spit upon my face
Turning aside God's own mercy
Tramping down his saving grace"

Then the heavenly vision lifted
All my darkness turned to light
I knew my record was clear in Heaven
An innocent prisoner in God's sight

1980

<u>*Only God*</u>

Only God could make a Christmas
By the birth of his Son
Only Angels could bring the message
That the world's Savior now had come.

Only God in love and power
Could make a star so bright
To light the way to the manger
Where Christ was born that night.

Only God could place those shepherds
In the quietness of that hour
To see the great transaction
Of Heaven's glory, then in power.

To hear earth's greatest message
Sweetest words ever spoke to man

Salvation for the human race
In God's redemption plan.

In the angels life giving promise
When the shepherds heard them say
"I bring you tidings for all people
A Savior is born to you this day."

December 1981

<u>*God's Christmas Message*</u>

What a beautiful morning that must have been
In God's time so long ago
When his Angels broke all silence
And the Heavens became all aglow

What sacred presence they must have felt
When the Angels begin to sing
When the humble shepherds heard their voices
With the great tidings they did bring

The greatest message ever spoken to earth
"A Savior has been born"
God's great love for the soul of man
Was now to be known

God could not look upon his creation
See the soul he put in man
Deceived and kept in Satan's bondage
Without a choice in a redemption plan

So he chose Mary for a virgin mother
To bring forth his only begotten son
To shed his blood, give his life, die on a cross
To bring redemption for everyone

So in these closing days upon this earth
For the year of 1992
May that message again break all silence
"A Savior has been born to you"

May God's great message be rehearsed
"Peace on earth, good will towards man"
May it again break all of sins barriers
To bring salvation to every land

December 1992

<u>*My Christmas Greeting*</u>

Another year is passing quickly
With its many nights and days
Life with its joys and cares and changes
With many experiences along the way

Life's road not always been full of pleasure
Not always with roses blooming sweet
Many times there were some problems
Some of them been hard to defeat

But I have seen your smiles, heard your laughter
I have seen your tears to
In all these things I've shared my love
With each one of you

May some word that I have spoken
Or maybe just a smile that I gave
Has made your pathway a little brighter
For you to remember this Christmas day

Yes there are faces we will not see
There are voices we will not hear

But they left us memories that will brighten
These vacant places with Christmas cheer

But many are the blessings to be remembered
That was shared across the earth
May in love they be remembered
In honor of our Savior's Birth

May our pathways be enlightened
With blessings of Christmas morning
May our hearts be filled anew
With God's sweet love and anointing

Play harp
I see Jesus in a manger
I see Jesus in Bethlehem
I see Jesus I see Jesus
I see Jesus in Bethlehem

Read at my Sunday school class

1993

Christmas Thoughts

Today I sit here in my home,
Many thoughts cross my mind
Another year is passing fast,
It's another Christmas time.

Across the world bells are ringing,
Christmas Carols are being sung,
In the cities homes and village
Pretty lights have been strung.

Everywhere the spirit of Christmas,
Has spread its wings of love
And the shadow brings a sacredness,
There's a sound from above.

Not a new song or another message,
Just the one heard that night
When the angels came from heaven,
And the star, shone so bright.

Just the same divine presence,
That hovered over the earth
When the angels brought the tidings,
And told of our savior's birth.

A message born, when earth's foundation
Was in the very beginning of time,
When God made salvations plan,
For the souls of all mankind.

To this world he sent his son,
Born in a virgin birth
To live and die on a rugged cross,
To save lost souls, throughout the earth.

So, today I close my thoughts, rejoicing,
I have heard the message all anew,
The same sweet tidings when Jesus saved me,
"A Savior has been born, for you."

1978

My Special Christmas Greeting - 1983

To all of you at the Macks Creek Clinic
Who works so patiently every minute

Caring and sharing with problems and ills
In so many lives to rebuild

Many thoughtful words, a smile or two
Has meant so much from all of you

Your thoughtfulness perhaps has often meant
Half a cure for aches that we present

Many times your smile or a word of cheer
Fell so softly in my listening ears

Perhaps erased from a troubled mind
An ache where nothing else could find

So many times at close of day
You to, had grown weary along the way

From others problems you helped to solve
But in understanding you did resolve

To say a word in kindest terms
To troubled minds who did yearn

For just a touch that you cared
And your time with them shared

May our Heavenly Father above
Out of the abundance of his love

Reward you this Christmas season
With all good things that are pleasing

Caring and sharing each new day
Just as you care for others along the way

Christmas

I have searched for words to put together in a wish I want to say,
That would express my appreciation I have for all of you today.

I have seen your smiles, heard your laughter, perhaps been times I've seen your tears
You have shared your love and kindness with me all thru the years.

Perhaps you never knew how much I cared or how much you've smoothed my way
So that's why I've tried to find words to share my love and wishes for you this Christmas Day

May your Christmas season be full of sunshine with many showers of love and prayers
May your pathway be brightened with the friendships that many shares.

As we greet this another Christmas morning in the closing year of 1995
May our hearts again rejoice in the message "a savior has been born to you"

A Christmas Message

Time is swiftly passing by
Another year will soon be gone
We now are seeing the Christmas season
Across the world in another dawn

But what does Christmas mean to us today
With world conditions as they are in

Wars, hatred, lust, greed for power and gain
Cults and every immoral sin

In all the blackness thru out the earth
Is there any light for us to see
Is there any hope or assurance
Any love and peace for you and me

Where is there light and hope and peace
From whence does it come
Have we forgot that great transaction
In the birth of God's own son

Have we forgot that humble manger
Where the Christ child was born
Have we forgot the Angel's message
That gave us our first Christmas morn

Have we failed to see his star
Such light never known to man
As it shone over that lowly manger
Parting darkness in every land

When all heaven was aglow
With God's message to this earth
As the Angels sang and proclaimed it
Of the Savior's humble birth

Yes, there is light, peace and hope
From whence does it come
From the great love of God
When he sent to earth his begotten son

Saying "Glory to God in the highest"
Peace on earth, good will toward man

A Savior to you has been born
Salvation has come to every land

Yes, there is victory for our world
There's a message to be heard
There's a need of turning back to God
"I am the way, the truth, and the life," says his word

Yes, there is a message to all people
In every place, where souls may be
Will it be accepted in repentance
In these closing days of 1993

Read at church

1993

Untitled Work, No Date (4)

Just wouldn't be natural I reckon
If I wasn't around to say
My little happy greeting
For your Christmas Day

So I've made it sweet and very spicy
With special ingredients thru and thru
And every wish is special flavored
For a special friend like you

*Wealthy at the former home of Ola Cross near
Montreal, Missouri*

Untitled Work, 1995

I have searched for words to put together
In a wish I want to say
That would express my appreciation
I have for all of you today

I have seen your smiles, heard your laughter
Perhaps been times I've seen your tears
You have shared your love and kindness
With me all thru the years

Perhaps you never knew how much I cared
Or how much you've smoothed my way
So that's why I've tried to find words
To share my love and wishes for you this Christmas day

May your Christmas season be full of sunshine
With many showers of love and prayers
May your pathway be brightened
With the friendship that many share

As we greet this another Christmas morning
In this closing year of 1995
May our hearts again rejoice in that message
"A savior has been born to you and I"

A Christmas Greeting

I wish I could send to each of you
A greeting card or a gift or two,
Or say a word in a special way,
That would make you happy on Christmas day.

Wish I could take you by the hand
Or say something so you'd understand,

That from the depths of this heart of mine,
I share my wishes all good and fine.

So when you read this little greeting
You'll know it's me just a speaking,
My Christmas wish right in your ear,
And it's for every one of you to hear.

So to all of you across the way,
May you have a Merry Christmas day
And may the coming year bring for you,
Health and joy, all the way thru.

The Christmas Message

Herald out to the world the glad tidings again,
A Savior is born to the children of men.

The angels that sang to the shepherds that night,
Yet sing in the glory in the glory of His birth and life.

"Glory to God in the highest," they say,
A Savior was born in a manger of hay.

Thru ages this message has ever been true,
Bringing peace on earth and happiness, too.

To a world in strife and sorrow and shame.
The Bethlehem star shines bright again,

Lighting the way thru darkness and sin,
To peace on earth, good will to men.

September 1992

My Christmas Greeting(2)

I cannot send to each of you,
A personal card and line,
But this little verse is meant for all,
Just everyone so fine.

It's my heart's very best in wishes,
If you're here or far away,
I want to share in the true Christmas spirit,
With you this Christmas day.

I want to lift my eyes to Heaven,
My soul in Him be hid,
The son of God who was born on earth,
A manger for a crib.

And may this great Christmas season,
Bring glad tidings to every one,
Peace and good will to all the world,
Thru the Christ Child, God's own son.

Christmas Thoughts

Today, I sit here in my home
Many thoughts cross my mind
Another year is passing fast
It's another Christmas time

Across the world bells are ringing
Christmas carols are being sung
In the cities, homes and village
Pretty lights have been strung

Everywhere the spirit of Christmas
Has spread its wings of love

And the shadow brings a sacredness
There's a sound from above

Not a new song or another message
Just the one heard that night
When the angels came from Heaven
And the star, shone so bright

Just the same divine presence
That hovered o're the earth
When the angels brought the tidings
And told of our Savior's birth

A message born, when earth's foundation
Was in the very beginning of time
When God made salvations plan
For the souls of all mankind

To this world He sent His son
Born in a virgin birth
To live, and die on a cross
To save lost souls, thru out the earth

So today, I close my thoughts, rejoicing
I've heard the message all anew
The same sweet tidings when Jesus saved me
"A Savior has been born for you"

Dedicated to all my friends everywhere

December 13, 1984

Christmas Blessings

May the joys of Christmas blessings
Be renewed day by day

May the New Year unfold a brightness
On each step along our way

May new thoughts and inner vision
Fill our hearts rich and sweet
As we share them with others
May all be blessed, with those we meet

As we see the old year ending
The only peace we can find
Is in the heart of God's children
Like those of yours and mine

With this assurance for you and me
Knowing there is love, hope and life
May the New Year find us faithful
Sharing with others, God's love and light

Farewell to 1996

As I fold the old year calendars
And laid them all aside
There were so many memories in them
With mixed feelings I looked at them and cried

My walls looked so bare and empty
With new calendars I now have replaced
But memories that are laid aside
The coming year cannot erase

The stain of tears may be on some pages
In the calendars now laid away
Perhaps when I wrote with trembling hand
Some special memory for that day

But thru all the joys and cares of life
Whatever they have been
May I be richer in experiences
For a new year now to begin

Did I learn what lessons taught me
Thru many changes, sorrow, and pain
Did I learn to choose more wisely
And value life's more important things

Did I learn in the passing year
In life's uneven span
When many times I was confronted
With things I yet don't understand

So now as I step into a future
What it holds I cannot see
But God has laid the stepping stones
And marked each one he has for me

So let me find his words more precious
That he places in my heart
As they give me the security
For the promises they impart

Now let me greet the coming year
With lessons I have learned
Let my faith be strengthened
For the future to now I turn

Let me feel the nail scars plainer
In the touch of the master's hand
As he leads me thru the places
Where my feet cannot stand

Let me find his words more sweeter
When I hear him say to me
"I'll never leave you, nor forsake you"
By your side I'll always be

Now as I step from the closed door
Of the old year of 1996
Let me be worthy of innocent tears
For the many memories that exist

And as I launch out into a future
Facing life's storms whatever they be
I yet will have that nail scared hand
To hold and guide and pilot me

A Tribute to the Old Year

Another year is gone from my vision
The Master of time has closed the door
But let me bow my head in reverence
As I see a new year dawning for 1994

Let me not forget the blessings
In the past year of my life
In whatever changes there has been
And whatever has been the price

God's love has been a lamp light
For every step that I have made
His love has been my strengthening
He has heard every prayer that I prayed

Whatever words that I have spoken
Whatever deeds I have done
God has them recorded in his memory
For whatever reward I have won

Whatever failures I have suffered
Whatever mistakes I have made
God's Holy Spirit has been my teacher
And made corrections when I prayed

So now another year has come and gone
That shared with me its length of time
May God's purpose been accomplished
In his gift of love and blessings he chose to be mine

So now as I stand again on life's door step
Facing another future I cannot see
Let my faith continue to be strengthened
To hold and guide and pilot me

A New Year Resolution

God knows how to soothe all our sorrows
He knows how to dry all our tears
He has a way to give us comfort
And to guide us thru all our fears

Some time we fail to hear his still small voice
Or feel the touch of his hands
And our footsteps become entangled
In life's pathway on slippery sand

Some time we have to pay a price
For things we unwisely choose
Because Satan's price tags looks so simple
That he presents to me and you

Then in these moments of our weakness
And when our faith is not released

Satan removes his price tags
And takes the advantage to deceive

As we now open the New Year's door
And take our first steps there in
May our love, faith, and trust in God be strengthened
To keep us free from Satan's sins

Play on harp: "My Faith Looks Up to Thee"

1994

<u>*That's for the Year of 1993*</u>

Again I have folded the old year calendars
And laid them all aside
With many memories I will recall
Of happy days and times when I cried

But thru all the joys and cares of life
Whatever they have been
May I be richer in experiences
For a new year to begin

Did I learn what lessons taught me
Thru changes, sorrow and pain
Did I learn to choose more wisely
And value life's more important things

Did I learn in the passing year
In life's uneven span
When many times I was confronted
With things I yet don't understand

Did I learn to be more thankful
For those who stood by my side

To help lift in my burdens
And share in tears when I cried

So now as I step into a future
What it holds I cannot see
But God has laid the stepping stones
And marked each one he has for me

So let me find his words more sweeter
That he places in my heart
May they give me the security
For the promises they impart

Now let me greet the coming year
With lessons I have learned
Let my faith be strengthened
For the future, to now I turn

Let me feel the nail scars plainer
In the touch of his hand
As he leads me thru the places
Where my feet cannot stand

Let me find his words more sweeter
When I hear him say to me
"I'll never leave you, nor forsake you
By your side I'll always be"

Another year is gone from my vision
Its closed door I can see
And again I stand on life's threshold
Facing the new year of 1993

And as I launch out into a new future
To face life's storms, what e're they be

I yet will have that nail scared hand
To hold and guide and pilot me

My New Year Greeting

Another year has passed so quickly
With its many nights and days
Life with its joys and cares and changes
With many experiences along the way

Life's road not always been full of pleasure
Many decisions we had to make
Sometimes we made them unwisely
And had regrets for our mistakes

But may some word that we have spoken
Or maybe just a smile we gave
Has made some ones path a little brighter
For them to remember this new year day

Yes, many times I have heard your laughter
I've seen your smiling faces to
I've known of your deeds of kindness
In the things I have seen you do

Many times I have seen your tears
As you wiped them from your face
In the love and sympathy you were sharing
For others, sorrows to be erased

May some word or deed of kindness
That we have shared with someone else
Has lifted a burden that was too heavy
For them to bare or overcome by them self

Yes, there are faces we will not see
There are voices we will not hear
But they left us memories that will brighten
The vacant places in the coming new year

May all of God's blessings be remembered
That has been shared across the land and sea
Where ever there has been a harvest of salvation
And lost souls have been set free

May all of our pathways be enlightened
As the new year unfolds this morning
May our hearts be renewed and filled
With God's sweet love and anointing

Read at church

1995

A Tribute to the Old Year

"My Country Tis of Thee", play harp.

The old year was sitting in his office
Completing records for the year '85
He knew the hours were passing fast
The new year would soon arrive.

He wanted his records to be complete
Ready to meet the tests of time
For all of life's great principles
He had stood for, and underlined.

As he slowly closed his finished books
He reverently bowed his head

Folded his hands upon his desk
In trembling words, he said.

"All the records now are sealed
History's memory covers the earth
May the power of God's salvation
Renew in hearts of the Saviors birth."

In memory he could hear resounding
The Bible message to every hand
"Unto you, a Savior has been born
Bringing peace on earth, good will toward man".

He said, "This to will be my message
I leave recorded in '85
May it be heard and received
If our nations are to survive".

The old year arose feebly to his feet
Footsteps heard soft and low
The new year was just arriving
The old year, now must go.

Stepping from the stage of time
his heart had mixed feelings
In every land there was hatred
Deep wounds that needed healing.

He knew thru centuries in the past
God's love had been spurned
Mankind had sought for selfish power
From righteousness they had turned.

As the old year made his final step
This message he spoke in love

"There's hope and peace for any people
Thru faith and trust, in God above".

Birthdays

A Tribute to my 86th Birthday

Perfection has always been my goal
That I've strived for all my life
But there were prices to be paid
Some time battles I had to fight

Responsibilities often became a burden
With problems I could not solve
Cares and worries became so many
My life they entered and involved

After living thru 86 long years
There's been many steps I have made
There's been many changes I have seen
But life's final diploma holds my grades

But thru all the many things in my life
That I yet don't understand
But God who planned my 86 years
Has never failed to let go my hand

As I reach the end of my life's journey
May the grades that I have attained
Be worthy to promote me to that new life
With perfection where I can live again

A Tribute to my 87th Birthday

Birthdays are such happy days
Till they get to be so many
When eye sight fails, hair gets gray
And we get all faded and skinny

When life's problems get more heavier
Our memory starts to slipping

Familiar names we forget
Our nerves start to skipping

But Let us make the best of every day
With life that God has given
For he has promised a perfection
With a new life with him in Heaven

Untitled Work, June 30, 1996

88 long years ago today I was born
In my mother's arms I was placed
Just an innocent baby girl
With life's 88 years I must face

Life has been just a schoolroom
Each day with lessons I had to learn
Made mistakes many times to be corrected
That brought regrets in return

Cares and problems I often faced
Decisions I had to make
Many times I made them unwisely
Had to suffer for my mistakes

But one day in my life's schoolroom
A great message there I heard
It taught me about God's great love
Salvations plan in his word

In my heart it was accepted
With peace and joy it did unfold
Jesus became my Lord and teacher
And the savior of my soul

When I step from this life's schoolroom
May the grades I have attained
Be worthy to promote me
To that new eternal life again

Where years will not be numbered
No more death will ever come
But eternities promise will be fulfilled
Where new eternal life will have just begun

Play on Harp

Blessed Assurance Jesus is mine
Oh, What a fore taste of Glory divine
Heir of salvation purchase of God
Born of his spirit and washed in his blood
This is my story, this is my song
Praising my Savior all the day long
This is my story, this is my song
Praising my Savior all the day long

June 30, 1996

<u>A Tribute to my 89th Birthday</u>

My birthdays were such happy days
In the years that have gone by
But now old age has took their place
With its changes, pains, and cries

My steps are unsteady
My eye sight getting dimmer
My memory getting out of gear
My hair all gray and thinner

Some time we are criticized
For things we do and say
By those you yet don't understand
That our old age is on its way

But I will admit very kindly
That I am learning fast
That old age is overtaking me
And my life on earth, soon be past

But I pray, the many years I have lived
In this life were not in vain
And in that great resurrection morning
I can step out, to live forever again

1997

<u>*In Honor of my 89th Birthday*</u>

June 30th 89 years ago I was born
In my mother's arms I was placed
Just as innocent little baby girl
With a long future I must face

Today I stand on this new 89th year threshold
Facing a future I cannot see
Life with new experiences
Perhaps is waiting now for me

But as I stand on this new year threshold
My mind goes back thru memory's lane
I go thru days of fun and laughter
Thru days of sorrow and of pain

I go thru days that had decisions
That were hard for me to make

Some perhaps I made unwisely
That later proved was a mistake

I go thru my happy school days
Childhood days without a care
Responsibilities that had less meaning
Dad and mother, and brothers were there

Family ties then were unbroken
That hurt of sorrow long I never knew
Our days together had newer meaning
The years seemed happier too

But as I return thru years of memories
Reliving days I hold so dear
Where I learned life's many lessons
To guide me thru life's many years

Yes, life has been a school room
Thru experiences I have been taught
The meaning of life's true values
Were not achieved without a cost

So all the years that are past and gone
I have not lived in vain
With many experiences and great faith
I'll meet my remaining future with lessons gained

1997

*Wealthy at the former home of Ola Cross near
Montreal, Missouri*

Untitled Work, No Date (5)

Yes, my life holds many changes
As I look back thru 90 years
I've had days happy with laughter
I've has days with pains and tears
I've had days with sunny skies
I've had days with storms and rain
I've had days with health and happiness
I've had days with hurts for tears and pain
But thru it all God has been good
Giving me birthdays for 90 years
May I accept it now with greater faith
As I face it today, as it appears
May I be remembered by each of you
For something I said or done
That will always be a blessing to you
In your days that are yet to come.

Untitled Work, No Date (6)

Birthdays are such a pleasure
When we are young and free
But may all your birthdays be a pleasure
Regardless of how many years you see

Your joints may begin to get arthritis
With pain here and there
Your memory slips a cog or two
Some gray streaks get in your hair

May have to change your glasses
Your eye sight gets a little dim
Maybe your hearing not so good
Birthdays start getting less popular then

But after all they say old age
Is the crowning part of life
So may you accept each new birthday
Regardless of what may be the price

Untitled Work, No Date (7)

My clock of life in this world
Was set many years ago
Thru 90 years of life in this world
For experiences to face and know

My life's grades are not forgotten
In God's great book of life
Thru many joys and grief's and sorrows
When I had to pay a price

But my faith that has sustained me
I will reap my reward
When I step out in his eternity
In that new life promised by my Lord

Happy Birthday

I have tried so hard to find
Just the right words to say
That would express my heart's best wishes
For you on this special day

Then I thought, "well what the use
Just use the old familiar phrase"
One that's expressed the hearts true feeling
Down thru life's many days

So again, I will repeat them
With three little words so true

One's thoughts filled with all good wishes
When I say, "I love you

My birthday wishes for you today
Could not be counted, measured, or weighed
To express the meaning and worthiness I have
For the wonderful person you have made

A wife, a mother, and neighbor
A Christian example to
In all life's problems that came along
You seemed to know just what to do

Your smiles were filled with sweetness
Your words had meaning to
So in all my birthday wishes
May they be filled with love for you

May many happy years yet be yours
With blessings along the way
I am sure a reward will be waiting
When time has ended on your birthdays

Love always, Aunt Wealthy

Birthdays

For us, birthdays are not a keepsake
To lay upon a shelf
they are to be shared with others
Who have birthdays like our self

We like to share our friendships
Our joys and cares and age
Some time even get our picture
On the county's paper page

How ever, though our birthdays
Some time get a little bit unkind
And causes us to get old looking
Like this 85th birthday of mine

Our hair gets thin and grayer
Our eye sight a little dimmer
Our memory starts forgetting
Many things we can't remember

After all, may the many years
That God has given me to live
May his purpose been accomplished
Made me worthy of another eternal life to live

June 8, 1993

Birth date June 30, 1908

Best Wishes

As usual I do not have a greeting card
With all the fancy frills and tucks
With pretty flowers, birds and kittens
With verse and rhymes and all that stuff

Really they do mean so much
And brightens up the days
When we open an envelope
And are greeted in such lovely ways

But knowing you as I do
In your sweet poetic mood
And as we have things so much in common
I know you won't be rude

To get my plain simple greeting
That comes right out of my heart
Fresh and fragrant and sincere
Its beauty to impart

Remembering You in 1994

Birthdays are just a part of life
From cradle to the grave
With 12 months in each year
With life's experiences, God has gave

Life is just a school room
Just one day at a time
Each year gives us its diploma
With the birthdates of yours and mine

Time brings age and many changes
We learn from experiences great and small
Many disappointments blight our happiness
Discouragement causes many a fall

Only God holds the thread of life
Knows each number of our days
But time will come this thread be broken
And close life's number on our birthdays

But as you look back thru all the years
With their joys and cares and tests
May this birthday today you are having
Be remembered as one of your best

September 1994

Family and Friends

A Mother's Love

If a mother's heart were like a book
With pages opened wide
And we could read it page by page
I'm sure we'd be surprised

We'd find the things that caused her hair
To turn into its gray
We'd find why the wrinkles on her face
Seemed to deepen day by day

We'd see tears streaming from her eyes
As she cried in secret prayer
When life's burdens grew too heavy
And no one seemed to care

We'd wonder why her smiles could be
So tender and so sweet
How could she patch up all our troubles
And with patience, each day meet

We'd wonder how she could ever endure
In giving her best in life
Smoothing the way for those she loves
What ever be the price

Dear old mothers, with graying locks
With lines across your brow
Your life is a beautiful story
An ever blooming flower

Of all the things that God did make
That was pure and divine
He chose the best there was in life
To make your mother and mine

And when Heaven's gates swing open
And we climb the golden stair
I'm sure a mother's love
Will greet her loved ones there

Our Mother

Mother was first to break our family circle
December 19 the year of '47
How well I remember that morning
When God took her soul to Heaven

Such a sadness gripped all our hearts
Such an emptiness came in our home
When we saw our mother pale and lifeless
Such sorrow, we had never known

The brightness of the sun that morning
Was dimmed by our tears and grief
For only crying in those sad moments
Could we find a touch to bring relief

To us our mother was so precious
Her love so kind and sweet
The thot of going on with out her
Was almost more than we could meet

But thru the lonely days that faced us
Thru many years that has come and gone
Time has had a way to heal the sorrow
But left sweet memories to linger on

And with assurance in God's great promise
That we will meet our mother again

Has soothed the tenderness in our hearts
In the scars made by sorrows pain

April 5, 1983

<u>*In memory of my mother and in honor of all you mothers here today.*
I dedicate my thots to all of you.</u>

When my pathway seems so narrow
When dark clouds hover low
It's there I need my dear mother
To show me how I should go

When the sunsets grow so darkened
And I need a spark of light
It's then I need my dear mother
Who knew how to part the night

When I need advice in my problems
When I need a friend that is true
When I need a love that's warm with Heaven
And only a mother knew

When life itself some times seems stranded
On a stormy shore of time
Its then the guiding hand of mother
Her child, longs to find

But while my days must pass with out her
Yet there's something left to guide
Her advice and hear examples
That I learned by her side

How she sheltered in her dark hours
Under God's protecting wing

How in love, faith, and patience
In steadfastness she would cling

So thru the years that make my journey
And in trials I have not met
Let me have the faith that caused my mother
To be a mother I can't forget

And when my path grows so narrow
And dark clouds hover low
Its then I'll have my mother's Savior
To show me how I should go

In Memory

*In memory of my mother, Betty Rainwater who passed away
December 19, 1947.*

I think of that sunny December morning,
When God called mother for our home,
How sorrows clouds overshadowed,
And we all were left so alone.

To us she was so good and kind,
Each day was brightened with her face,
Thru all the years she has been gone,
No one has ever filled her place.

And now again in sweetest memory,
My heart renews in love,
For my precious, dear, sweet mother,
Who is waiting for me in Heaven above.

Her daughter, Wealthy Calvert, Montreal, MO.

Memories

Many years ago before I was born
A baby brother was called away
In his birth, his little life was taken
He never knew the dawn of day

My mother's arms had never held him
No name to him had been given
His little voice had not been heard
Too soon, death's angel took him to heaven

Yes, thru many times, thru many years
I've wondered why he had to go
Just an innocent little baby
No life on earth for him to know

But then again, at a later time
A little sister I never knew
Suddenly died in my mother's arms
She was about the age of two

In those days of diphtheria illness
Little ones it seemed to choose
And then often with little warning
Their life then they had to lose

Very little I ever knew of the sadness
These little ones left in my home
Just the things I learned from the neighbors
In the years long after I was born

But I was told the grief of my mother
Was so heavy for her to bear
But the neighbors helped to carry her burden
Till it was lifted with their love and care

No, I don't remember seeing my mother's tears
I never heard her talk about her grief
But I know in the sweetness of my mother
God cared and healed in relief

Time and years went on its way
Now a teenager in the Lord I believed
I had read of guardian Angels
And their visits that had been received

One day my mother and I were in our garden
And these words I heard her say
"I dreamed last night that little Elfie
Lighted on my shoulder and then she flew away"

So quickly came an answer to me
And to my mother I did say
"That was little Elfie's guardian Angel
That God has sent to you today"

Mother so often dreamed of flying
And perhaps in these dreams
Little Elfie's Angel was present
A sweet comfort to her to bring

If this was God's way of choosing
In the deaths of these little ones
His purpose will be rewarded
When his wisdom in this life is won

Perhaps these little guardian Angels
Are watching over my path each day
And sends me words of inspiration
That I share with others along my way

Yes, I must say there's many things
In this life I will never understand
Till I walk and talk with Jesus
And feel the touch of his hand

But I am sure God had a purpose
And all was done in his great love
He knew he'd need some guardian Angels
To send to earth from up above

From little lives that had never been blighted
Had never had the stain of sin
Had never felt the guilt in conscience
With the hurt from worldly things

But yonder in God's great wisdom
In that bright resurrection morn
These little one's life will be restored
Who dies at birth or soon after they were born

Thru the many years that followed
Many times I heard my oldest brother tell
Of the sweetness of that little sister
That he remembered and loved so well

In that brightness of that resurrection morning
Perhaps all silence will be broken
In a praise from little Angel's voices
Whose words on earth were never spoken

1995

Mother's Love

In honor of my dear mother and in honor of all mothers that are here today. I share with you my thoughts.

God placed the rainbow in the clouds
Its beauty we all can see
He placed the stars in the sky
To twinkle for you and me

He placed the fragrance in the roses
For all who pass it by
He made all the little birds
To sing for you and I

He made a love so rich and sweet
Something that was divine
So he made a mother
And called her yours and mine

Upon her face she placed a smile
To greet us day by day
From her lips the sweetest words
No other one could ever say

He gave her an understanding
A tenderness to soothe our pains
Just something about our mother
Takes care of life's many things

Only God could place such love
Where it would never die
The noblest gift in all the world
To share with you and I

It was in his great creative plan
In the very beginning of time
When he chose a place for his love
In hearts of mothers like yours and mine

Mother

Back through the years with sorrow and tears
Mother, with a heart of love
Stood by to guide her little ones
With patience known only above

We do not know our Mother's trials
The tears that she had to shed
We do not know the story
Of the gray hairs on her head

Yet we do know that our Mother's love
From the depths of her heart
Is painted on our vapor of life
And with time will never depart

The precious lessons that Mother has taught
Her advice that was never wrong
Will stand before us in our future
Long after Mother has gone

Untitled Work, 1953

As I stand beside the grassy mound
That marks my mother's grave
Embraced in earths cold bosom
Her silent body lays

A helpless form cold and lifeless
Returned back to the clay
Leaving behind a life of memories
As it walked and talked one day

But I look away from earths embrace
Oh why do I weep

When a part of God's creation
Has only gone back to sleep

The real mother that I knew
Will return again some day
And live again in this temple
That will be changed from its clay

Its sting of death has been conquered
Her eternal victory has been won
The grave for her will be empty
Thru her faith in God's dear son

Her soul that's now in God's presence
The real mother that I loved
Will someday walk and talk with me
In the glories of Heaven above

Where there will be no more sad partings
No more life's ties to be break
But we will know each other better
In a love words never spake

The years between since she left me
Will forever be erased
And the tenderness of God's love
Will dry the tears from my face

So as I stand beside the grassy mound
Where my mother's body in death sleeps
I can't help but look above
To a place with golden streets

There I hear the voice of Jesus
I go to prepare a place

And in one of these mansions
I'll see my mother's face

Perhaps it won't be long now til we will meet
In that bright resurrection morning
Where there will be no more sad partings
In God's eternal home coming

For My Companion Egbert Calvert

His day of work on earth was over
Life's battles all are o'er
With his trust in the risen Lord
He has crossed over to Heaven's shore

His soul that God saved and loved
Was ready for its flight
To its upward home above
Just beyond our sight

We look beyond the mound of clay
Where his body will quietly sleep
We look above to God's bosom
A paradise so sweet

Where the soul of our loved one
Rejoices in Heaven's eternal dawn
Where some day we can meet again
In that great resurrection morn

1953

Wealthy with her husband (Thomas) Egbert Calvert

To Our Beloved Pastor

We will get a little more older and
Our hair a little more gray
Our bodies will get a little more weaker
During the time you are away

There'll be some changes made here
And there and around
Maybe some chairs become vacant
And a few new made mounds

But midst all the tears and heartache
And whatever comes our way
We know somewhere our faithful shepherd
Yet loves us and cares and prays

Thru all the storms and tides and
Seasons there comes a sunny sky
For God has promised his dear Children
He'd always be standing by

So we look beyond this parting
As you leave your flock behind
Trusting there are others for his number
That he is sending you to find

So all the things that we will meet
And have to face alone
We'll walk side, beside each other
In the love to us you have shown

And thru all the changes that may come
While our shepherd is away
Our love for you will just grow sweeter
Till you return to us someday

If by chance this parting should forever
Break the chain of earthly ties
We'll still be looking forward to that morning
When we meet together in the sky

When the great master Shepherd
Makes the roll call for his own
Gathering us all together in his sheep fold
To live forever in that Heavenly home

Read to Brother Horace McDaniel in his last service at the Richland Assembly of God Church (1928).

<u>Christian Friendship</u>

Our Christian friendship that
Only God could design
And permitted us to share
Together and enjoy in so sweet a time
But the sacred and the sweetness
Of this friendship will be
Rewarded and cherished
During the rest of my life's time
Perhaps in Gods time of
Eternity in that new life
On some golden street, we will
Meet and clasp hands again,
In that new life of friendship sweet.

August 7, 1996

<u>Untitled Work, January 6, 1999</u>

Brother Mac another year of Christian friendship
That you and I so long have known

But now perhaps there may come changes
In the new year that's coming on

Age, health, and strength in our bodies
With its time may over come
Life its self may be lifted
And our days together done

But yonder in God's great memory
In eternities book of life
He has our names written down
And holds the reward in a new life

Where there will be no more partings
No more sickness or growing old
No more heart aches to mar the happiness
In God's eternity that he unfolds

Untitled Work, August 7, 1996

May your body find the sweetest rest
In a comfort you long have not known
May your nights be filled with sweetest sleep
In your sleep at night in your home

May this pillow come to bless you
That I am sending you today
May it be a blessing in comfort
That God has prepared for you today

To Brother Mac

In Remembrance

Happy are the many memories
Of the past days that are gone

When it seemed my cares were few
And never very long

But life must make its changes
With many things we can't forget
But our faith in God will be remembered
And let us know he loves us yet

Yes there has been many changes
Thru the long life he's gave you and me
But thru faith in God's great love
Our togetherness in friendship will forever be

A copy was sent to Brother Mac in March 1999. Thoughts and good advice will go a long ways.

My Dear Sister in Law Clarice Rainwater

Our loved ones life has been chosen
Death's angel has called her name
Her soul was carried away in silence
In that appointed moment when it came

She was ready for that appointment
Her name was written down
In God's great mind of remembrance
When in life, his salvation, she had found

Her life was filled with love and kindness
For her family and her friends
Her example in her Christian living
Will have reward in a new life again

We did not hear the angels whisper
Just a quietness was all we knew

Its presence left an emptiness
Her life had been taken then we knew

My Dear Sister-in-Law Poem

Our loved ones life has been chosen
Death's angel has called her name
Her soul was carried away in silence
In that appointed time when it came

She was ready for its message
Her name was written down
In God's great mind of remembrance
When in her life, his salvation she had found

Her life was filled with love and kindness
For her family and her friends
Her example in Christian living
Will have reward in the new life to begin

We did not hear the angels whisper
Just a quietness was all we knew
Its presence left an emptiness
Her life had been taken, then we knew

Our tears cannot erase our sadness
Nor the memories we hold so dear
But God's great love can sustain us
In a comfort in the loss of one so dear

But in his word is his promise
I'll never leave them, nor forsake
Your burdens I have carried
Your griefs on Calvary's Cross I did take

Clarice Rainwater and Wealthy, Sisters-in-Law

Love's Sustaining Power

In life while walking down my pathway
I've come to hills that were steep to climb
I've come to valleys so deep and narrow
My path was hard to find.

I've felt my strength begin to weaken
In steps I was not sure
Many times fears have seized me
When my path seemed insecure.

When I could not see for obstructions
That tangled 'round my feet
And the goal I sought in achievement
Could have ended in defeat

When my faith could have faltered
And my trust broke in despair
My hopes and inner vision
Dimmed be the weight of cares

But thru the years I have learned
In my most trying hour
There was a hand that touched me
With love's sustaining power

A hand with scars that were made
When Jesus hung on Calvary's tree
Thru life's journey they have guarded
Over hidden paths I could not see

In memory of my father who has been gone for 30 years and in honor of all you fathers who are here today, I share my love and these thots with you today.

What is Home Without a Dad

My home now seems so vacant
Upon this Father's Day.
For its only been 3 months ago,
Since he was called away.

Since that last sad morning,
As we stood at his bed,
Saw him in the hands of death,
And heard the words he said.

How he told us he was going,
In his heart there was no fear,
How he'd placed his faith in God,
For deaths moment that was near.

Time has passed by so quickly,
We all have been so sad.
For home is not the same,
With out our dear old dad

So many places where we look,
We miss him being there,
As the table when we eat,
His empty room, his vacant chair.

But God how much we'd miss,
The ones we loved so dear,
And he made a way to comfort,
And sweeten bitter tears.

H e left us with a promise,
That we could meet again,
Where there'd be no more parting,
No sickness, grief, or pain.

So I rest in that assurance,
And when my heart is so sad,
I find comfort in that promise,
I'll again see my dad.

In Heaven's eternal meeting place,
What a glorious time that'll be,
Fore ever with my mother and dad.
Their face, I can always see.

1955

Untitled Work, No Date (8)

We don't understand dad's lengthy suffering,
Or the pain he felt in his flesh,
We only know God gave him the strength,
To sustain him in such distress.

There seemed so little that we could do,
As we watched by his side,
Only our love, hope, and faith,
Helped ease the pain he bore inside.

That bleeding hand on Calvary's cross,
Once felt each suffers pain,
And in the hours we helpless stood,
God's strength flowed out again.

As we saw his hours of suffering,
We know that great hand divine,
Touched him and gave him the patience,
That we witnessed so many times.

He was ready for his summon,
He was ready for that rest,

That comes when death gives release,
Folds our hands upon our breast.

He was ready to greet the morning,
On that bright eternal shore,
Where hope and life and gladness,
Are his forever more.

And God has given us his promise,
That soothes in grief's deepest pain,
In that great resurrection morning,
We can all meet again.

Wealthy with her father, Everette Rainwater

God Has Promised

In memory of my dear father, who passed away March 3, 1955. I dedicate my thot's today. May God's rich blessings be for every father that's here this morning on this special day.

Many times my heart must suffer sorrow
In a grief that seems so hard to bear
But I have learned to look thru my tears
With a faith that comes thru prayer

Thru this faith, I see nailed scarred hands
Nailed yonder on a wooden cross
My Savior bleeding and dying alone
Whose pains has comfort for my every loss

At the foot of his cross, in faith I kneel
There, my heart feels a touch of healing
From the drops of blood that are falling
From his wounds that are bleeding

Then again I find a comfort
As I see him kneeled in prayer
In the quietness of Gethsemane garden
Facing his painful crucifixion hour

In these great moments of intercession
I believed he called my name
In his great love, grace, and mercy
He shared my losses and every pain

There in my heart he placed a comfort
As he died on Calvary's cross
Where he paid for all my sins and sorrows
Gave me a faith to sustain in every loss

There he promised, "I'll never leave thee'
In troubles I'll hear your cry
In sorrow I'll be your comforter
Thru life I'll be by your side

I'll be a light upon your pathway
When sorrows, tears blind your eyes
My love will find its way to healing
In life's many broken ties

For Your Anniversary

Sweet are the memories
That linger thru the years
Of days you've spent together
Sharing joys, sorrow and tears

Now, as you've reached the golden years
In the journey of your life
Today may your vows be renewed
In happiness, as man and wife

And, as you journey on together
Till you reach life's setting sun
And night spreads around you
And parts your way, one by one

But God has another future
And a place of eternal life
And he holds the vows of his children
Who became as man and wife

He has reserved their happiness
Anniversaries will have no end
For in that new Heaven and new earth
Eternal happiness will just begin

Honoring Mr. and Mrs. Bob Pruitt
"God bless you"

In Memory

In memory of my companion, George Green, who passed away
January 13, 1969.

Time does not seem to be erasing,
From my memory of that sad day,
When death's angel came in my home,
And took my dear companion away.

Two long years have passed and one,
Just day by day they passed me by,
Days and nights that were full of sadness,
Heartaches, and tears in my eyes.

Our home has such a vacant place,
No smile to cheer us any more,

No one to help us in our problems,
No one to greet us at the door.

But some day, we'll meet him again,
In Heaven's beautiful place,
We'll know the sweetness in his voice,
And see the smile upon his face.

Sadly missed by his companion, Aileen Green and children.

Friends

I'm so glad for all my friends,
They make my life worthwhile,

Their warm hand clasp and words of cheer,
Their always friendly smile.

They keep the dark clouds brushed away,
They keep my pathway clear,
For when I come to narrow ridges,
I find them standing near.

Like the rose that flings its fragrance,
Out on every little breeze,
To share its sweetness with the passers,
That's what my friends meant to me.

"In Memory", written by request for Larry Leathers in memory of his companion who died January 3, 1983.

Today I stood in my doorway
A spring breeze cooled my face
Song birds were singing every where
Flowers were blooming every place

All of life seemed responding
To the happy touch of spring
The blight of winter seemed forgotten
It's drabness gone from every thing

Yet there was such an emptiness
That time had not erased
From the depth in my heart
Where a sadness had been placed

Memories of other happy days
With my companion by my side
Seems to bring a loneliness
I just can't forget or be denied

Side by Side we walked together
Happy hours spent in our home
With our children we laughed together
Love and happiness was all our won

But one day, God in his wisdom
Called our loved ones name
And took her home to Heaven
Just why we can't explain

He knew our hearts would be lonely
But his comfort he would share
He promised he'd never leave us
For us he'd always care

And some day he will tell us
Why he called her home
When we can better understand it
How he loved and cared for his own

We wait in that sweet assurance
That we can be together again
In that beautiful place called Heaven
No more parting, no more tears or pain

Written for Betty Grady

In precious memories we rehearse
Thru many years of time and care
With family ties yet unbroken
Together we love, cherish and share

We look beyond the scars of life
Graying hair and tottering feet
We honor each one who are so blessed
To keep our family ties complete

To achieve our 5th generation
We count it such a joy
When a precious one was added
Now, a two year old happy boy

Mother

To Girtrue Grady

The clock had struck its morning hour
The day had just begun
When mother heard her homeward call
Her work on earth was done.

She was ready for the summon
And in the quietness of the dawn
God reached his hand and touched her
And chose to take her home.

We do not think of her as dead
Her soul just slipped away
Went back to God who gave it
In a better place to stay.

Its house of clay, flesh we loved
Now sleeps in Sweetest rest
No aches or pains or worries
Nothing to molest.

Reflections

Life's Reward

Too long I have been alone with life's problems
Some that has been too heavy for me to bare
Many times I stand in need of some ones help
But there are not many who seem to care

Always to busy to lend a hand
Or even stop when passing by
Not time now days for us old folks
Just let us root hog or die

Many times I have shared in favors
In the cold and heat and rain
If I could bring a smile to some ones face
My reward was in their gain

But too soon the roses that we give
Just wilt and petals fall away
Their sweet fragrance is soon forgotten
That meant so much to them one day

But yonder in that new life for me waiting
I'll hear the words of my dear Lord
"The many kindnesses you done for others
Are now awaiting your reward"

September 12, 1994

Old Age

They say old age brings beauty
So why worry then I say
If the face gets some wrinkles
And the hair gets some gray

If our memory slips a little
Eye sight a little dim
Our steps a little slower
With arthritis now and then

Both most folks pass us by
Because we are so slow
They don't see much beauty in us
Because we are getting old

Us old widows get so grouchy
We'd never find a man
They say we are so childish
Our ways they couldn't stand

So old age may not have its beauty
But I am here to say
It has had a lot of tearing down
In so many different ways

Perfection Has Reward

Whatever things in life I done or chose
I wanted them to be exact and straight
For I had an eye to see perfection
In whatever I done or tried to make

Thru life's journey there's been testings
Many times thru answers I never learned
But thru the mistakes I made unwisely
Yet for the perfection I had that yearn

When I dwell in that new Heavenly city
Where the streets are paved with gold
Where no sickness or death ever comes
And where no more will I grow old

And there in that new life again
God who has kept my records and my grades
I'll find in him that perfection
That in my life on earth I always craved

July 9, 1998

Life's Road

The road thru life I am traveling on
I will someday come to its end
My purpose is this life will be fulfilled
A new future be waiting for me then

Life has been just a school room
Each day with lessons I had to learn
Made mistakes many times to be corrected
That brought regrets in return

Cares and problems I often faced
Decisions I had to make
Many times I made them unwisely
Had to suffer for my mistakes

But one day in my life's school room
A great message there I heard
It taught me about God's great love
Salvations plan in his word

In my heart it was accepted
With peace and joy it did unfold
Jesus became my Lord and teacher
And the Savior of my soul

When I step from this life's school room
May the grades I have attained

Be worthy to promote me
To that new eternal life again

October 26, 1991

Life's Pathway

Many times the journey thru this life
The one that has been assigned to me
Is not always paved in smoothest roads
Nor thru gardens, where flowers I see

Many times theres a cross for me to carry
Or a sacrifice I must make
Or sorrows I must bear
Till it seems my heart will break

Many times I grow tired and worried
With so many hills to climb
They seem so steep, all around me
Till my way, is hard to find

But I have learned to pause and look
Beyond these highest hills
See a hand out stretched to me
From a cross, where blood is spilled

So thru my journey in this life
How ever rough my path may be
I know the scars in my Saviors body
Has felt all suffering first for me

He was mocked, despised and hated
Hung on a rugged cross to die
With nails drove in his hands
A sword pierced his side

His feet has walked each lonely pathway
Seen every tear upon my face
Each time I'd fall or stumble
He lifted, by his tender embrace

My Eternal Hope

In my long life I've been given
There are many memories I recall
Of happy days with youth and laughter
When it seemed I had no cares at all

When my problems I knew how to solve
Oh yes there were times I had to cry
But there was always a hand to touch me
To guide my steps as they passed by

So now after all my long years of life
I know my days on earth will soon be ending
But my faith I've kept in God so long
In his eternal new life, I will have its beginning

February 1998

In Memory of My Little Dog

If there is such a thing as a broken heart
That's the pain I feel today
For the vacancy of my little dog
Since death has taken him away

But I know he is not suffering
His little body feels no pain
But God will find a way to comfort
My broken heart once again

God could not look upon his suffering
But in his own special way
Sent a silent sleep to overcome him
His life was then taken away

All life has an appointment
That some time must come to an end
But let us bow in humble reverence
In God's comfort that he will send

In Memory of My Little Beanie Dog

Many times my heart has felt a brokenness
In a hurt I thought I could not bear
But in God's sweet love and infinite wisdoms
He had a comfort with me to share

If only my Beanie could have told me
How his little body hurt inside
Yet I was so helpless to bring a comfort
To soothe his pain when he cried

But God could not look on his suffering
Nor see the sorrow in my heart
So in his own mysterious way
Little Beanies life made its depart

Many things we will never understand
In the mind of God's great love
When life's purposes have been completed
With his touch from above.

He came into my yard one day, when he was a very small puppy and I named him Beanie. He was put to sleep January 19, 1996. He was about 10 years old.

Wealthy at home with her little dog Beanie in 1986

Christian Memories

Today I sit alone with memories
That cross life's many long miles to you
In that Christian fellowship thru many years
That I treasure today and review

I may soon feel that silent touch
That only deaths angel to me can give
As it lifts my soul in its flight
To heaven's place where I can live

I pray my life on earth these 87 years
Has brought blessings that God designed
And somewhere in his great endless future
I'll reap his reward for this life of mine

Early in life I accepted God's salvation
Thru faith and obedience in his name
Thru my long life with its many testings
His promised love I have gained

So today I sit alone with memories
That cross life's many long miles to you
Of our Christian fellowship on earth together
That I treasure today and review

July 18, 1995

In honor of my Christian pastor in the many years gone by, Brother Horace McDaniel (Brother Mac)

Thinking Moments

Many times I just sit down and think
Of some of life's many lovely things

Of a rainbow arched across the sky
After a warm summer rain

Of a big full moon over head
Erasing out the dark of night
Shining across so many lands
With its soft and mellow light

The different songs of birds I hear
As they fly among the many trees
Each one has its own designing
To build its nest among the leaves

The beauty that comes with the Spring time
With new life teaming all around
After a long dormant stay
In the winters frozen ground

The beauty in the rose and lilies
And in so many flowers that I see
They all seem to have a language
That their beauty reveals to me

Their fragrance seems to erase
If any bitterness that I feel
When in these moments I sit and think
And God's love is revealed

In the smile of innocent children
As they look into my face
I see something that God has given
Sharing his love and infinite grace

Beautiful sunsets at close of day
That I so often see

Reminds me of a fairer land
With loveliness for all eternity

The sacredness that surrounds me
When I talk to God in prayer
There's a beauty in his holiness
To know he is listening and he cares

On and on, I could never number
All of life's lovely things
That God has placed along my pathway
To erase the ugliness that trials often bring

August 1992

Untitled Work, May 3, 1998

This evening I set looking far to the west
Across the many miles so far away
I could see a blanket of moving clouds
Often hiding the sunset for my day

There was just a quietness everywhere
With a peep of the sun now and then
As the clouds silently moved away
And let a ray of sunshine in

Many memories crossed my mind
As I kept gazing so far away
I recalled the friendship of an old friend
Who lives far in the west, yet today

I thought perhaps he to see these clouds
As they gather over his Utah home
Not knowing they now bring me memories
Of an old friend that I long have known

Untitled Work, No Date (9)

The pace of time with all its advancements
Are becoming far beyond our limitations
The true values for the coming century
Will be absorbed by mans technology and intervention

The bounds of human experimentation
Will seem to have no end
With its sale price is for promotion
For future power for greed and gains

Human minds will be absorbed
With a wisdom that was never known
The laws of God will be abused
Many perhaps will become unknown

The lusts of sins will have new meaning
And become a way of life
Guilt will be erased by lust and fashion
Conscience free, became the price

Scientific, technology invades our generation
With its limit to deceive
Satan again will try to restore his promises
That he first made in Eden's garden to Eve

However all these hastened changes
Are being fulfilled in technologies mind
But Gods warming have been made known
In the very days of our time

Satan again has took advantage
With his wisdom and his pride
For greed and gain and lust and power
God's laws are being shoved aside

The mind of men has become absorbed
For a knowledge beyond his power
And Satan has again took advantage
And wickedness is the reward for this hour

But the people who are called by Gods name
And are inspired by his love
And have received his gift of salvation
Have been redeemed by Christ shed blood

Childhood Memories

Today I sit alone and thinking
My mind goes back to childhood days.
To the old home down in the valley,
The place where I was raised.

So many places there I yet remember.
That's yet so dear to my mind.
That brought a happiness I can't forget.
Ones, nowhere else, I'll ever find.

A valley, so green and shady and cool.
Hills where grapes and berries grew.
Nuts and acorns were everywhere.
There were lots of flowers blooming to.

There birds built among the trees,
And sang at early dawn.
They seemed to greet you like a friend,
To cheer you all day long.

The old cave spring, its clear cold water.
Of it I often think.

And the pitcher full of lemonade,
Oh, how good it was to drink.

We never knew any other refrigeration,
Except out at the spring,
Where we had a place built in,
And there we stored about anything.

Yet these are just a few of the memories,
That cross my mind today,
As I think of my old home place,
In the valley not far away.

Where my family circle was unbroken,
With happy days around the home,
Where friends and loved ones often gather,
No one seemed sad, or alone.

But the scenes there are changed now,
Like around any old home place,
But memories of the days gone by,
Time and decay, cannot erase.

School Day Memories

When I pass be my old school building,
Tho' now a home, remodeled all anew.
Memory, takes me back to childhood,
Before my school days were thru.

That old school room, once I loved,
The lessons that were taught,
Noon hours with play and games,
And the fun that they brought.

From day to day with patient teachers
Laying down stepping stones
Ones, that thru the years I don't regret,
I was privileged to walk upon.

Molded into my life, principles
That were noble, true and pure
Those that have helped me thru the years
Life's better things, for me insured.

Oh, if I could be a child again,
Just for a year and a day,
And study my lessons all over,
Enjoy those games at play.

Those happy school days; no cares to blight,
When all went like a song
Too soon the bell ceased ringing,
And those happy days were gone.

School mates and pals that I loved,
Many have passed away,
But precious are the childhood memories
That I cherish yet today.

Others with families, all with homes
Their faces I would not know
Some I will never meet again
Oh! How life changes so.

But sweet memories still will linger,
To bridge the space between
Of happy childhood school days
Whatever changing years may bring.

Wealthy (Calvert) Rainwater

Just to Sit and Think

Many times I sit down and just think
Of some of life's many lovely things
Of a rainbow arched across the sky
After a warm summer rain

Of a big full moon overhead
Erasing out the dark of night
Shining across so many lands
With its soft and mellow light

The different songs of birds I hear
As they fly among so many trees
Each one has its own designing
To build its nest among the leaves

The beauty that comes with the springtime
With new life teeming all around
After a long dormant stay
In the winters frozen ground

The beauty in the rose and lilies
And in so many flowers that I see
They all seem to have a language
That their beauty reveals to me

Their fragrance seem to erase
If any bitterness I may feel
When in these moments I sit and think
And Gods love is revealed

In the smile of innocent children
As they look into my face
I see some thing that God has given
Sharing his love and infinite grace

Beautiful sunsets at close of day
That I so often see
Reminds me of a fairer land
With loveliness for all eternity

The sacredness that surrounds me
When I talk to God in prayer
There's a beauty in his holiness
To know he is listening and he cares

On and on I could never number
All life's lovely things
That God has placed along my pathway
To erase the ugliness that trials often bring

In Remembrance

Happy are the many memories
Of the past days that are gone
When it seemed my cares were few
And never very long

But life must make its changes
With many things we can't forget
But our faith in God will be remembered
And let us know he loves us yet

Yes there have been many changes
Thru the long life, he's gave you and me
But thru faith in Gods great love
Our togetherness in friendship will forever be.

March 1999

Memory's Lane

Today I stand on the threshold
Facing a future I cannot see
Life with new experiences
Perhaps is waiting now for me

As I stand on this new year threshold
My mind goes back thru memory's lane
I go thru days of fun and laughter
Thru days of sorrow and of pain

I go thru days that had decisions
That were hard for me to make
Some perhaps I made unwisely
That later proved was a mistake

I go thru my happy school days
Child hood days without a care
Responsibilities had less meaning
Mom and dad were there to share

Family ties then were unbroken
The hurt of sorrow I never knew
Our days together had newer meaning
The years seemed happier too

But as I retrace thru memories lane
Reliving days I hold so dear
Where I learned life's many lessons
To guide me thru each coming year

Yes life has been a school room
Thru experiences I've been taught
The meaning of life's true values
Are not achieved without a cost

So all the years that past and gone
I have not lived in vain
With experience and greater faith
I'll meet my future with lessons gained

Sept 15, 1998

When I Don't Understand II

There's so many things in this life
That I will never understand
But I know the wisdom of God's mind
Has everything in his plan

I wonder why in fondest dreams
In hopes that are built so high
They just seem to come with the morning
With evening shades they blight and die

I wonder why the bliss of friendship
Must end at the grave
Voices we loved so soon are hushed
Why does it have to be this way

I wonder why we cannot hold
The song birds as they sing
Why we can't retain the fragrance
Of the lilies of the Spring

But with all the whys of this life
There comes to my mind
A reproof from God's wisdom
A knowledge that is divine

I look back to that Eden garden
Where Satan made the scar

Where God made his first call to man
"Adam, I want to know where you are"

The choice of human mind was made
The whys of life begin
Disobedience brings forth its fruit
Thru time to days we now are in

But as I search in God's great wisdom
In the depths of his love I find
His great plan of salvation
To redeem your soul and mine

Alone With Memories

Today I just sat thinking
I felt lonely and depressed
My mind began to fill with memories
Of other days, their happiness

I thought how the changing years
Had left so many scars
How so many dreams had been blighted
So many hopes and been marred

I thought of those happy days in school
When life was young and free
The greatest problem I thought I had
Was making all those E's

So many schoolmates now are gone
Very few I can call to mind
Who sat beside me in the classes
Reciting lessons, time after time

I thought of my dear companion
Who once walked by my side
Together we shared the things of life
We worked, we laughed, we cried

I thought of so many friends
I had known thru the years
Of happy hours, we had spent together
We shared our love, our joys, our tears

I thought of years with my family
My childhood days at home
When life seemed to have less problems
We had a happiness all our own

After all the hours of thinking
I realized the past was gone
But I found a comfort in the memories
Of the happiness, I once had known

I call these thoughts for today,
My Memorial Contribution

Memories are bridges beautiful and wide
Spanning thru life's years of time
Pillard and cabled in the depths of hearts
Like those of yours and mine

Memories of a dear old mother
As she braved the stormy years
Conqueror of honor, praise, and love
Thru many trials and bitter tears

Baby's angelic prattling voice
Its kiss and sweetest coo

Are treasured with the little toys
With memories sweet and true

A sweet heart soldier one who crossed
The stormy sea to war
Bled and died on the battle field
To return to us no more

Happy gatherings 'round the old fireside
With dad and mother and all
Where family ties were then complete
The family circle not broken at all

That envelope sealed with a lock of hair
A picture with a smiling face
Tucked away with tear drop stains
A memory is there, time cannot erase

Those old love letters hidden away
Yellow with age and faded
Many childhood sweet heart dreams
Are written on those pages

Summer vacations ending too soon
Loved ones gone from our side
Plans we made, but they fell apart
Like castles built on tossing tide

Memories are bridges, spanning the years
Where joys and sorrows cross
Painted them, folded on pages of time
Touches from life to never be lost

March 3, 1998

Life's road that I have traveled on so long
I am now coming to its end
It's journey has took me thru many changes
Thru many experiences I have been

Yes, there will be things to be remembered
Maybe something some one heard me say
That will continue to be an inspiration
To some one along their way

So many things that I have done
Will soon be forgot
When my footsteps are heard no more
But please, "just forget me not"

But God holds the key to eternity
Where we shall live again
And in his great resurrection morning
Our new life together will just begin

Along Life's Journey

Some time the journey in life seems long,
Our path grows weary, our feet seem worn,

The upward grades are hard to climb,
Our heart grows faint, our steps decline.

The days are long with restless nights,
The sky less blue, the sun less bright.

We think the rest of the world is gay,
Their path full of roses every day,

But when we reach where sunbeams fall,
And talk with others along the trail,

We soon will find that their lot too,
May be much darker than you knew.

It's not always the smile upon the face,
That reveals the heart of the human race.

Not the merry laugh floating down the aisle,
Not always as joyous, just all the while,

Heads bowed down in sorrow, smile thru tears.
We see the smile and count it all cheer.

Like the rose bush growing beside the way,
There's a thorn for every rose they say.

Our savior was sad and bitter tears shed,
His path too was hard to tread.

And as we pattern after the great living guide,
He always helps us over the tide,

Our hearts are made stronger in faith and love,
When we see his footsteps leading from above,

And we see the good Jesus in the garden of prayer,
With no one to wait with him in the dark hour.

But darkened hours passed and Heaven shone thru,
Bringing an immortal lesson for me and you.

So when the dark clouds cross our fairest sky,
Remember the sun will shine again, by and by,

Though the paths of others look smooth to tread,
Their dark clouds too may by low overhead,

So let weep and smile and pray,
Help bear each other's burdens along the way.

Galatians 6:2

Solitude

As I travel along life's crowded aisles,
A million things I meet,
Broken dreams and shattered hopes,
Nothing seems quite complete.

But when my heart feels most discouraged,
And the way seems rough and long,
I'm glad in solitude's garden
That I can walk alone.

Listening to little warbling melodies,
As song birds pass me by,
Feel the waxen silky petals,
Of flowers that are soon to die.

Hear the babbling of the brook,
As it lazily winds it way,
O're soft moss covered pebbles,
Thru grass and mints and spray.

Oh blissful garden of solitude,
I'm glad I found the key,
That unlocks me to the wonders,
Of being alone in thee.

Where I can mingle with nature's arts,
In an atmosphere divine,
Where the wavelengths of Heaven,
Are never hard to find.

Where I can have an immortal peace,
Under the shadow of His wing,
Where I can view a glimpse of Heaven,
And hear the Angels sing.

Oh, this wonderful garden of solitude,
To thee I love to flee,
And leave my worldly cares behind,
when burdens are too heavy for me.

What Do I Have in Hand

Many times I wish I had the voice
To sing like folks that I have heard
Or could play like some do in music
Or preach like some do God's word.

Perhaps there are some very good reasons
Just why I cannot do those things
Maybe I've never had the training
For results, that practice brings.

But I think of that great true story
In the Bible where I've read
Of the two little fishes
And the five loaves of bread.

How Jesus fed all those people
Who were hungry when they came
They all did eat, and were filled
And twelve baskets of food remained.

From this story I have learned
More about his sufficient grace
And I hear him say in my soul
There's no one else to take your place

So let me hide behind the cross
And what ever I have in hand
Let me use it for his honor
Not to please my self or man.

Just let me stay in the shadows
At the foot of the cross
In my heart an intercession
For some ones need or who is lost.

And what ever God has placed
In my hands for me to hold
May it be used for his glory
To bring him 5 or 10 or a hundred fold.

Scrapbook Remembrance

Perhaps soon I will have to put away
My pencils and papers all aside
Perhaps with stain of my tears
That fell as I cried.

But somewhere in some ones scrapbook
Some of my verses will be found
And my name will be remembered
In my writings I left behind

In that new life I will understand
The meanings of my poems
As I walk and talk with Jesus
And his voice to me be known.

Afterword

"The fragments of this book are threads from a life that has loved a span of time in this world. Our minds are gardens of thots. God gave us a privilege to reach life's highest standards, provided channels where in we could develop them. Too often the mind of human beings follow after material, shallow things and never wait to hear that still small voice of divine intelligence.

What the world offers us is merely the ashes of the genuine; and to taste the essence of the manna is life itself, we must remain in the channel where God created us, as mankind. Be still and wait upon our calling. Rise to that place, where we can see over the horizon of earth's carnal minded things and catch that glimpse and taste that sweetness of the true value of life. We will never really love in this great world, until we let loose of self, and mold our character in the divine will of our creator."

Love always
aunt wealthy

Made in the USA
Lexington, KY
10 March 2019